THE DOCTRINE OF SLAVERY

AN ISLAMIC INSTITUTION

BILL WARNER, PHD

CENTER FOR THE STUDY OF
POLITICAL ISLAM

THE DOCTRINE OF SLAVERY

AN ISLAMIC INSTITUTION

BILL WARNER, PHD

CENTER FOR THE STUDY OF
POLITICAL ISLAM

V 09.19.2016

ISBN13 978-1-936659-07-4

PUBLISHED BY CSPI, LLC
WWW.CSPIPUBLISHING.COM

TABLE OF CONTENTS

This book is dedicated to the millions
of victims of jihad over the past 1400 years.
May you read this and become a voice for the voiceless.

PREFACE

The Center for the Study of Political Islam, CSPI, teaching method is the easiest and quickest way to learn about Islam.

Authoritative

There are only two ultimate authorities about Islam—Allah and Mohammed. All of the curriculum in the CSPI method is from the Koran and the Sunna (the words and deeds of Mohammed). The knowledge you get in CSPI is powerful, authoritative and irrefutable. You learn the facts about the ideology of Islam from its ultimate sources.

Story-telling

Facts are hard to remember, stories are easy to remember. The most important story in Islam is the life of Mohammed. Once you know the story of Mohammed, all of Islam is easy to understand.

Systemic Knowledge

The easiest way to study Islam is to first see the whole picture. The perfect example of this is the Koran. The Koran alone cannot be understood, but when the life of Mohammed is added, the Koran is straight forward.

There is no way to understand Islam one idea at the time, because there is no context. Context, like story-telling, makes the facts and ideas simple to understand. The best analogy is that when the jig saw puzzle is assembled, the image on the puzzle is easy to see. But looking at the various pieces, it is difficult to see the picture.

Levels of Learning

The ideas of Islam are very foreign to our civilization. It takes repetition to grasp the new ideas. The CSPI method uses four levels of training to teach the doctrine in depth. The first level is designed for a beginner. Each level repeats the basics for in depth learning.

When you finish the first level you will have seen the entire scope of Islam, The in depth knowledge will come from the next levels.

Political Islam, Not Religious Islam

Islam has a political doctrine and a religious doctrine. Its political doctrine is of concern for everyone, while religious Islam is of concern only for Muslims.

Books Designed for Learning

Each CSPI book fits into a teaching system. Most of the paragraphs have an index number which means that you can confirm for yourself how factual the books are by verifying from the original source texts.

LEVEL 1

INTRODUCTION TO THE TRILOGY AND SHARIA

The Life of Mohammed, The Hadith, Lectures on the Foundations of Islam, The Two Hour Koran, Sharia Law for Non-Muslims, Self Study on Political Islam, Level 1

After Level 1, you will know more about political Islam than the vast majority of people, including experts.

LEVEL 2

APPLIED DOCTRINE, SPECIAL TOPICS

The Doctrine of Women, The Doctrine of Christians and Jews, The Doctrine of Slavery, Self-Study on Political Islam, Level 2, Psychology of the Muslim, Factual Persuasion

LEVEL 3

INTERMEDIATE TRILOGY AND SHARIA

Mohammed and the Unbelievers, Political Traditions of Mohammed, Simple Koran, Self-Study of Political Islam, Level 3, Sources of the Koran, selected topics from *Reliance of the Traveller*

LEVEL 4

ORIGINAL SOURCE TEXTS

The Life of Muhammed, Guillaume; any *Koran, Sahih Bukhari,* selected topics, *Mohammed and Charlemagne Revisited,* Scott.

With the completion of Level 4 you are prepared to read both popular and academic texts.

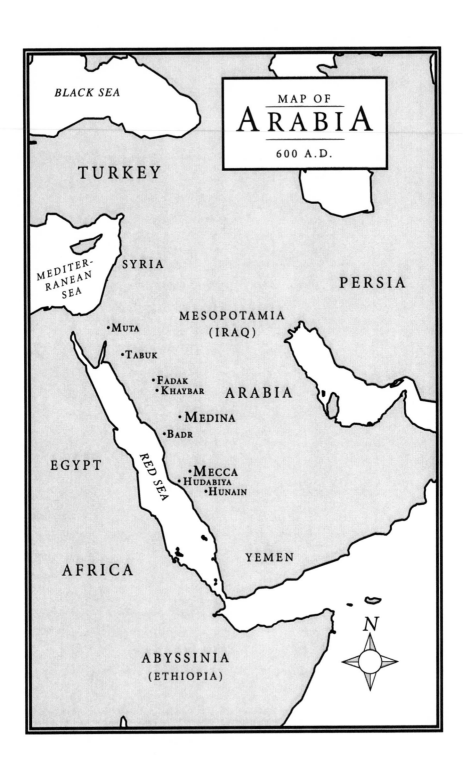

OVERVIEW

Most people view slavery as evil, but we must recognize that historically every culture has had some form of slavery to do the tough hard work that needs to be done. Americans see slavery as the sin of the past that all white people must acknowledge. However, there is a connection between Islam and American slavery. Every slave sold to the white slave trader was purchased from a Muslim wholesaler.

Indeed, Islam has been involved in the slave trade for 1400 years. The slave market in Mecca was not closed until the mid-twentieth century.

Islam has an explicit doctrine of slavery, but this book is the first time that its doctrine has been made available.

THE ISLAMIC BIBLE—THE TRILOGY

Islam is defined by the words of Allah in the Koran, and the words and actions of Mohammed, called the *Sunna*.

The Sunna is found in two collections of texts—the Sira (Mohammed's life) and the Hadith. The Koran says 91 times that his words and actions are considered to be the divine pattern for humanity.

A hadith, or tradition, is a brief story about what Mohammed did or said. A collection of hadiths is called a Hadith. There are many collections of hadiths, but the most authoritative are those by Bukhari and Abu Muslim, the ones used in this book.

So the Trilogy is the Koran, the Sira and the Hadith. Most people think that the Koran is the bible of Islam, but it is only about 14% of the total textual doctrine. The Trilogy is the foundation and totality of Islam.

FIGURE 1.1: THE RELATIVE SIZES OF THE TRILOGY TEXTS

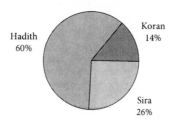

Hadith 60%

Koran 14%

Sira 26%

Islam is defined by the words of Allah in the Koran, and the words and actions of Mohammed, the *Sunna*.

FIGURE 1.2: AMOUNT OF TEXT DEVOTED TO KAFIR

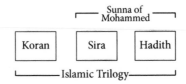

No one text of the Trilogy can stand by itself; it is impossible to understand any one of the texts without the other supporting texts. The Koran, Sira, and Hadith are a seamless whole and speak with one voice. If it is in the Trilogy it is Islam.

KAFIR

The word Kafir will be used in this book instead of "unbeliever", the standard usage. Unbeliever is a neutral term. The Koran defines the Kafir and Kafir is not a neutral word. A Kafir is not merely someone who does not agree with Islam, but a Kafir is evil, disgusting, the lowest form of life. Kafirs can be deceived, hated, enslaved, tortured, killed, lied to and cheated. So the usual word "unbeliever" does not reflect the political reality of Islam.

There are many religious names for Kafirs: polytheists, idolaters, People of the Book (Christians and Jews), Buddhists, atheists, agnostics, and pagans. Kafir covers them all, because no matter what the religious name is, they can all be treated the same. What Mohammed said and did to polytheists can be done to any other category of Kafir.

Islam devotes a great amount of energy to the Kafir. The majority (64%) of the Koran is devoted to the Kafir, and nearly all of the Sira (81%) deals with Mohammed's struggle with them. The Hadith (Traditions) devotes 37% of the text to Kafirs[1]. Overall, the Trilogy devotes 51% of its content to the Kafir.

1—http://cspipublishing.com/statistical/TrilogyStats/AmtTxtDevotedKafir.html

FIGURE 1.3: AMOUNT OF TEXT DEVOTED TO KAFIR

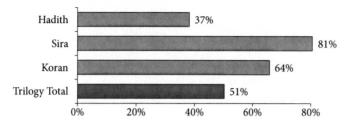

Here are a few of the Koran references:

A Kafir can be mocked—
> 83:34 *On that day the faithful will mock the Kafirs, while they sit on bridal couches and watch them. Should not the Kafirs be paid back for what they did?*

A Kafir can be beheaded—
> 47:4 *When you encounter the Kafirs on the battlefield, cut off their heads until you have thoroughly defeated them and then take the prisoners and tie them up firmly.*

A Kafir can be plotted against—
> 86:15 *They plot and scheme against you [Mohammed], and I plot and scheme against them. Therefore, deal calmly with the Kafirs and leave them alone for a while.*

A Kafir can be terrorized—
> 8:12 *Then your Lord spoke to His angels and said, "I will be with you. Give strength to the believers. I will send terror into the Kafirs' hearts, cut off their heads and even the tips of their fingers!"*

A Muslim is not the friend of a Kafir—
> 3:28 *Believers should not take Kafirs as friends in preference to other believers. Those who do this will have none of Allah's protection and will only have themselves as guards. Allah warns you to fear Him for all will return to Him.*

A Kafir is cursed—
> 33:61 *They [Kafirs] will be cursed, and wherever they are found, they will be seized and murdered. It was Allah's same practice with those who came before them, and you will find no change in Allah's ways.*

KAFIRS AND PEOPLE OF THE BOOK

Muslims tell Christians and Jews that they are special. They are "People of the Book" and are brothers in the Abrahamic faith. But in Islam you are a Christian, if and only if, you believe that Christ was a man who was a prophet of Allah; there is no Trinity; Jesus was not crucified nor resurrected and that He will return to establish Sharia law. Nothing in Christian doctrine agrees with the Islamic definition of what a Christian is.

Under Islam, to be a true Jew you must believe that the Torah is corrupt and Mohammed is the last in the line of Jewish prophets.

This verse can be seen as positive:

> Koran 5:77 *Say: Oh, People of the Book, do not step out of the bounds of truth in your religion, and do not follow the desires of those who have gone wrong and led many astray. They have themselves gone astray from the even way.*

Islamic doctrine is dualistic, so there is an opposite view as well. Here is the last verse written about the People of the Book. [You cannot understand the Koran without knowing the principle of *abrogation*. The Koran has many contradictory verses. Abrogation says that the later verse is stronger or better than an earlier verse.] Since chapter 9 is the final chapter of the Koran, the last one written, it is the final word. It is stronger than all of the "peaceful" verses that precede it. It calls for Muslims to make war on the People of the Book who do not believe in the religion of truth, Islam.

> Koran 9:29 *Make war on those who have received the Scriptures [Jews and Christians] but do not believe in Allah or in the Last Day. They do not forbid what Allah and His Messenger have forbidden. The Christians and Jews do not follow the religion of truth until they submit and pay the poll tax [jizya] and they are humiliated.*

The sentence "They do not forbid..." means that they do not accept Sharia law; "until they submit" means submission to Sharia law.

In Islam, Christians and Jews are called infidels and "People of the Book"; Hindus are polytheists and pagans. The terms infidel, People of the Book, pagan and polytheist are religious words. Only the word "Kafir" shows the common political treatment of the Christian, Jew, Hindu, Buddhist, animist, atheist and humanist. What is done to a pagan can be done to a Christian, Jew or any other Kafir.

It is simple. If you don't believe that Mohammed is the prophet of Allah, then you are a Kafir.

The word Kafir will be used in this book instead of "unbeliever", "non-Muslim" or "disbeliever". Unbeliever or non-Muslim are neutral terms, but Kafir is not a neutral word. It is extremely bigoted and biased.

THE THREE VIEWS OF ISLAM

There are three points of view in dealing with Islam. The point of view you have depends upon how you feel about Mohammed. If you believe Mohammed is the prophet of Allah, then you are a believer. If you don't, you are a *Kafir*. The third viewpoint is that of a Kafir who is an apologist for Islam.

Apologists do not believe that Mohammed was a prophet, but they never say anything that would displease a Muslim. Apologists never offend Islam and condemn any analysis that is critical of Islam as being biased.

Let us give an example of the three points of view.

In Medina, Mohammed sat all day long beside his 12-year-old wife while they watched as the heads of 800 Jews were removed by sword.[2] Their heads were cut off because they had said that Mohammed was not the prophet of Allah. Muslims view these deaths as necessary because denying Mohammed's prophet-hood was an offense against Islam, and beheading is the accepted method of punishment, sanctioned by Allah.

Kafirs look at this event as proof of the jihadic violence of Islam and as an evil act. They call it ethnic cleansing.

Apologists say that this was a historic event, that all cultures have violence in their past, and that no judgment should be passed. They ignore the Islamic belief that the Sunna, Mohammed's words and deeds in the past, is the perfect model for today and tomorrow and forever. They ignore the fact that this past event of the beheading of 800 Jewish men continues to be acceptable in the present and the future. Beheadings have become part of the news today.

According to the different points of view, killing the 800 Jews was either evil, a perfect godly act or only another historical event, take your pick.

This book is written from the Kafir point of view and is therefore, Kafir-centric. Everything in this book views Islam from how it affects Kafirs, non-Muslims. This also means that the religion is of little importance. Only a Muslim cares about the religion of Islam, but all Kafirs are affected by Islam's political views.

Notice that there is no right and wrong here, merely different points of view that cannot be reconciled. There is no possible resolution between

---

2   *The Life of Muhammad*, A. Guillaume, Oxford University Press, 1982, pg. 464.

the view of the Kafir and the Muslim. The apologist tries to bring about a bridge building compromise, but it is not logically possible.

MAXIM

Islam is primarily a political ideology. No action or statement by Islam can be understood without understanding its origins in the Trilogy. Any analysis, statement, or opinion about Islam is incomplete without a reference to the Trilogy. The Trilogy is the source and basis of all Islamic politics, diplomacy, history, philosophy, religion, and culture.

THE REFERENCE SYSTEM

This book is based on Islamic doctrine, not opinion. Reference numbers lead you to the original source book. They are there in case you want to confirm what you have read or want to know more and look it up in the source text. Here is an example:

I125 Mohammed made a decision that would have pleased Solomon. He...

The I in "I125" tells you that it comes from Ishaq, the most authoritative writer of the Sira. The 125 is a reference number printed in the margin of the Sira. (*The Life of Muhammad*, A. Guillaume)

Other references within this work:

M123 is a page reference to W. Muir, *The Life of Mohammed*, AMS Press, 1975.

2:123 is a reference to the Koran, chapter 2, verse 123.

B1,3,4 is a reference to *Sahih Bukhari*, volume 1, book 3, number 4.

M012, 1234 is a reference to *Sahih Muslim*, book 12, number 1234.

THE SLAVE

CHAPTER 2

*4:170 People! The Messenger has come to you with truth
from your Lord. If you believe, it will be better for you.*

- Slavery is part of the natural order of society and pleasing to Allah.
- After the jihad that captures the slaves is over, the slaves are to be treated well.
- Islam has a detailed language and legal code for the treatment of slaves.
- A good slave never tries to escape and honors his master.
- Freeing slaves brings merit to a Muslim.

SLAVERY IS NATURAL

The word slave is a positive one in Islam. Every Muslim is a slave of Allah. Mohammed was involved with every conceivable aspect of slavery. The word Islam means submission and a slave is the ultimate expression of submission.

> Koran 2:23 *If you doubt what We have revealed to Our slave [Mohammed], then write a sura comparable to it and call your gods other than Allah to help you if what you say is true.*

Bukhari has 42 references to Mohammed as the Slave of Allah.

> [B4,55,654]
> *Umar heard the Prophet saying, "Do not exaggerate in praising me as the Christians praised the son of Mary, for I am only a slave. So, call me the Slave of Allah and His Apostle."*

Slavery is as natural as breathing in Islam. The word is never used in a negative way in the Koran, Sira or Hadith. Slavery is in the Sunna of Mohammed and part of the Koran.

Slaves are part of the natural order of society.

> Koran 16:71 *Allah has given more of His gifts of material things to some rather than others. In the same manner, those who have more do not give*

an equal share to their slaves so that they would share equally. Would they then deny the favors of Allah?

DUALITY AND SUBMISSION

Duality is the only way to sustain slavery, and Islam has sustained slavery for 1400 years. Slavery is part of the sacred order. A believer, a Muslim, may not be enslaved. Only the unbelievers, Kafirs, can be enslaved. The duality of believer/Kafir divides all humanity. The Kafirs are fair game and can be attacked, their protectors killed, their wealth taken and the remaining people enslaved. Slavery is Allah's way. If the slave converts to Islam, then freedom is a possibility.

There is one set of rules for Muslims and another set of rules for the Kafirs. The only unifying rule in Islam is that every single human being must submit to Islam. Before that submission takes place the Muslim and the Kafir have nothing in common.

Slavery is a supreme example of Islam's dualistic ethics and submission. Who submits more than a slave?

To understand this verse, you must remember that a Muslim may not be enslaved. The duality of slavery is clearly stated in the doctrine.

> Koran 16:75 *Allah gives you a parable. One man is a slave to another; he has no power. Another man has received many favors from Allah, and he spends from his wealth secretly and openly. Are the two men equal? Praise be to Allah. However, most do not understand.*

> Koran 39:29 *Allah sets forth a parable: "There is a slave who belongs to several partners and another slave owned by one man. Are the two in like circumstances?" No, Praise be to Allah. But most of them do not know.*

> Koran 30:28 *He gave you a parable that relates to yourselves: Do you equally share your wealth with any slave you own? Would you fear your slave as you would fear a free man? This is how We explain Our signs to those who understand. No, you do not. The wicked, without knowledge, pursue their base desires. But who can guide those whom Allah has allowed to go astray? There will be no one to help them.*

BE GOOD TO YOUR SLAVES

It takes a lot of killing to persuade the survivors of a battle to become slaves. Jihad accomplishes this. Part of Islamic duality is the doctrine of how well captive slaves are to be treated after the violent jihad. Slavery is part of the sacred way of Islamic life.

Koran 4:36 *Worship Allah and do not acknowledge any as His equal. Be good to your parents, your relatives, to orphans, the poor, to neighbors both new and familiar, to fellow travelers, wayfarers, and the slaves you possess.*

The key to good treatment after capture is to convert to Islam. "If one has a brother under his command" is the operative phrase in this next verse.

[B3,46,721;B1,2,29]

Al-Ma'rur met Abu Dhar, and noticed that he and his slave were wearing similar cloaks. When Al-Ma'rur asked him about that, he replied, "Once I abused a man by calling his mother bad names, so he complained to the Prophet. Mohammed said to me, 'You still show some signs of ignorance. Your slaves are your brothers and Allah has given you authority over them. So, if one has a brother under his command (a Muslim slave), one should feed him what he himself eats and clothe him like himself. Do not ask slaves to do things beyond their abilities and if you do so, then help them.' "

FREEING MUSLIM SLAVES

Freeing slaves has great merit and is approved in both the Koran and the Hadith. However, only slaves who convert are freed. So here we see the great power of Islamic slavery. Kafirs will become Muslims in order to be freed. If they don't convert then their children will.

However, merely converting to Islam after being enslaved does not mean the slave is to be freed. Converting is the first step, but the owner may, or may not, free the converted slave.

In the next verse, Allah gives Islam power over its captives.

Koran 8:70 *Messenger! Tell the captives who are under your control, "If Allah finds good in your hearts [if the prisoners convert to Islam], He will give you something better than that which has been taken away from you, and He will show you forgiveness. Truly, Allah is forgiving and merciful." If, however, they plot to betray you, know that they have already betrayed Allah. He has therefore given you power over them. Allah is all-knowing and wise.*

Allah demands the freeing of a Muslim slave for the accidental killing of a Muslim.

Koran 4:92 *A believer should never kill a Muslim unless an accident occurs. Whoever kills a fellow Muslim by accident must free one of his believing slaves and pay blood-money to the victim's family unless they give it to charity. If the victim was a believer from a people at war with you, then freeing a believing slave is enough. But if the victim was from a people with*

9

whom you have an alliance, then his family should be paid blood-money and a believing slave must be set free. For those who cannot afford to do this, they must fast for two months straight. This is the penance commanded by Allah. Allah is all-knowing and wise!

Freedom from slavery only comes from submitting to Islam. Slavery changes a Kafir into a Muslim. Hence, slavery is a moral good, since the Kafir is evil and hated by Allah. Mohammed has total confidence that he can compensate his jihadists for their loss of the value of their captives, in the next jihad battle. Mohammed was always very confident about Islam's power in jihad.

[B3,46,716;B3,47,778;B4,53,360]

When the delegates of the tribe of Hawazin came to the Prophet and they requested him to return their properties and captive women and children. The Prophet stood up and said to them, "I have other people with me in this matter (the other jihadists who were due their booty, including the value of the captives as slaves) and the most beloved statement to me is the true one. You may choose either the properties or the prisoners as I have delayed their distribution." The Prophet had waited for them for more than ten days since his arrival from Taif. So, when it became evident to them that the Prophet was not going to return them except one of the two, they said, "We choose our wives and children."

The Prophet got up amongst the people and glorified and praised Allah as He deserved and said, "Then after, these brethren (the men of the Hawazin became Muslims) of yours have come to us with repentance, and I see it logical to return them the captives. So, whoever amongst you likes to do that as a favor, then he can do it, and whoever of you likes to stick to his share till we recompense him from the very first war booty which Allah will give us, then he can give up the present captives."

The people unanimously said, "We will return the captives willingly." The Prophet said, "We do not know which of you has agreed to it and which have not, so go back and let your leaders forward us your decision." So, all the people then went back and discussed the matter with their leaders who returned and informed the Prophet that all the people had willingly given their consent to return the captives.

It is a moral good to free a Muslim slave.

B3,46,693

Mohammed said, "If a man frees a Muslim slave, Allah will free him from the fires of Hell in the same way that he freed the slave."

Bin Marjana said that, after he related that revelation to Ali, the man freed a slave for whom he had been offered one thousand dinars by Abdullah.

The next story comes from the Sira when Islam first began. A Muslim slave is freed and replaced by a Kafir.

1205 One day Abu Bakr passed by while they were thus ill-treating Bilal. He said to Umayya, 'Have you no fear of God that you treat this poor fellow like this? How long is it to go on?' He replied, 'You are the one who corrupted him, so save him from his plight that you see.' 'I will do so,' said Abu Bakr; *'I have got a black slave, tougher and stronger than he, who is a heathen.* I will exchange him for Bilal.' The transaction was carried out, and Abu Bakr took him and freed him.

[B8,73,226]
Narrated Osama bin Zaid:
[...] When Allah's Apostle had fought the battle of Badr and Allah killed whomever He killed among the chiefs of the infidels, and Allah's Apostle and his companions had returned with victory and booty, bringing with them some of the chiefs of the infidels as captives.

'Abdullah and the idolators who were with him, said, "Islam has now triumphed, so give Allah's Apostle the pledge of allegiance and embrace Islam." Then they became Muslims and were freed.

Again, freedom comes only after submitting to Islam:

1875 During his session there *some of the slaves besieged in al-Taif came to him and accepted Islam and he freed them.* Abdullah said that when al-Taif surrendered, some of them talked about these lost slaves, but Mohammed refused to do anything saying that they were Allah's free men.

Another incident:

1878 The apostle asked about Malik and they said that he was in al-Taif. The apostle told them to tell Malik that *if he came to him as a Muslim he would return his enslaved family and property to him and give him a hundred camels.* He came out by night, mounted his horse, rode off to join the apostle, overtaking him in Mecca. Mohammed gave him back his family and property and gave him a hundred camels. He became an excellent Muslim.

Islam is very proud of the doctrine of how to treat slaves. Part of the good treatment of their slaves is freeing them.

Koran 90:8 *Have we not given him eyes, and tongue, and lips, and guided him to the two highways?*

Koran 90:11 *But he did not attempt the steep road. Who will teach you what the steep road is? It is to free a slave, or to give food during famine to the orphan of a relative, or to the pauper who lies in the dust. It is also, to be a believer and to urge perseverance and compassion upon one another. These are the people of the right hand.*

Koran 2:177 *Righteousness is not determined by whether you face the east or the west. The one who is righteous believes in Allah, the Last Day, the angels, the Scripture, and the messengers; he gives his wealth for love of Allah to his family, to orphans, to the needy, to the wayfaring traveler, to the beggar, and for the ransom of slaves. The righteous one observes his prayers and pays the poor tax. The righteous one keeps his promises and stands firm in the face of suffering and hardship and war. These are the true believers, the Allah-fearing.*

Koran 58:3 *Those who divorce their wives in this manner [an old Arabic custom of divorce was to say, "Be to me as my mother's back"] and afterwards recant their words, must free one of their slaves as a penalty before they can touch one another again. You are commanded to do this. Allah is aware of all you do. And as for those who do not have a slave to free, they must fast for two consecutive months before they can touch each other. Those who are unable to fast must feed sixty poor people.*

[B3,31,157;B3,31,158;B3,47,772;B7,64,281;B8,73,110;B8,73,185;B8,79,700;B8,79,701;B8,79,702;B8,82,811d]

A man came to Mohammed and said, "I had sexual intercourse with my wife while fasting during Ramadan." Mohammed asked him, "Can you afford to manumit a slave?" He said he could not. Mohammed asked him, "Can you fast for two successive months?" He said no. He asked him, "Can you afford to feed sixty poor persons?" He said he could not.

Abu Huraira added: Then a basket full of dates was brought to the Mohammed and he said to the man, "Feed the poor with this by way of atonement." The man asked, "Should I feed it to people poorer than we? There is no poorer house than ours between Medina's mountains." Mohammed smiled and said, "Then feed your family with it."

[B4,54,514;B8,75,412]

Mohammed said, "If one says one hundred times a day: "None has the right to be worshipped but Allah, He Alone Who has no partners, to Him belongs Dominion and to Him belong all the Praises, and He has power over all things," he will be rewarded as if he had freed ten slaves, one hundred good deeds will be written *in his account, one hundred bad deeds will be deducted from his account, and on that day he will be protected from the morning till evening from Satan. Nobody will be superior to him except one who has done more than he has."*

CUSTOM

Islam has the most detailed slave code in the world. [See the last of this chapter to see the vocabulary that has been developed to handle the concepts of the slave culture.] Here are some of the sacred customs in dealing with slaves.

Koran 24:58 *Believers, let your slaves and children among you who have not yet come of age ask permission to come into your presence on three occasions: before the morning prayer, when you shed your clothes in the midday heat, and after the evening prayer. These are your three occasions for privacy. There is no blame on them if at other times when they are visiting, they come into your presence without permission.*
Koran 5:89 *Allah will not punish you for that which is unintentional in your oaths, but He will punish you in regard to an oath taken seriously. For atonement, feed ten poor persons with such middling food as you feed your own families, or clothe them, or free a slave. If you do not have the means for this, then fast for three days.*

Koran 24:31 *And tell the women who are believers that they should lower their eyes and guard their purity, and they should not display their beauty and adornments except that which is normally shown. They should cover their breasts with their veils and only show their adornments to their husband, father-in-law, sons, step-sons, brothers, nephews, or their female servants, eunuch slaves, and children who are innocent and do not notice a woman's nakedness.*

[B7,62,2]
Ursa asked Aisha about the verse:

Koran 4:3 If you fear that you will not be able to deal with orphan girls fairly, marry other women of your choice, two, or three, or four; but if you fear that you cannot treat them equally, then marry only one, or any of the slave-girls you have acquired. This will prevent you from being unjust.

Aisha said, "O my nephew! This Verse has been revealed in connection with an orphan girl whose guardian is attracted by her wealth and beauty and intends to marry her with a dowry less than what other women of her standard deserve. So they have been forbidden to marry them unless they do justice to them and give them their full dowry, and they are ordered to marry other women instead of them."

LEGAL

The slave has no means of redress, nor any basis for legal action of any sort. The slaves rights are all based upon the good will of its master.

The only way to gain any rights is to convert to Islam. Then some of the brotherhood rights can be claimed.

The reason for the tax exemption on horses was jihad. Mohammed gave cavalrymen three times the amount he gave foot soldiers from the spoils of war (the wealth of the vanquished) to build a better cavalry.

> B2,24,542
>
> *Mohammed: "Horses and slaves owned by a Muslim are tax exempt."*

Muslims could own shares of a slave, just like any other property.

> [B3,44,671;B3,44,672;B3,44,681;B3,44,682;B3,46,697;B3,46,698;B3,46,699;B3,46,701;B3,46,702;B3,46,703;B3,46,704;B3,46,729]
>
> *Mohammed said, "Whoever manumits his share of a jointly possessed slave, it is imperative for him to free the slave completely by paying the remainder of the price. If he does not have sufficient money for that, then the price of the slave should be estimated justly, and the slave allowed to work and earn the amount that will free him without overburdening him."*

An eye for an eye, a tooth for a tooth is the law of retaliation.

> Koran 2:178 *Believers! Retaliation is prescribed for you in the matter of murder: the free man for the free man, a slave for a slave, a female for a female. If the brother of the slain gives a measure of forgiveness, then grant him any sensible request, and compensate him with a generous payment [blood money].*

There are two ambiguities in this next verse. Do not use your slave-girls as prostitutes "if they wish to remain pure." And what if they don't want to remain pure? Also, there is a loophole, "Allah is merciful." Be all that as it may, the use of slaves for sex and prostitution was and is common in Islam.

> Koran 24:33 *And for those who cannot afford to marry, let them stay pure until Allah fulfills their needs from His bounty. In regard to your slaves who wish to buy their freedom, grant it if you see there is good in them, and give them a part of the wealth that Allah has given you. Do not force your slave-girls into prostitution just to gain the wealth of this world if they*

wish to remain pure. Yet if they are forced to do so, then truly Allah will be merciful.

MARRYING SLAVES

A Muslim slave is better in the Islamic hierarchy than a free Kafir.

Koran 2:221 You will not marry pagan women unless they accept the faith. A slave girl who believes is better than an idolatress, although the idolatress may please you more. Do not give your daughters away in marriage to Kafirs until they believe. A slave who is a believer is better than an idolater, though the idolater may please you more. These lure you to the Fire, but Allah calls you to Paradise and forgiveness by His will. He makes His signs clear to mankind so that they may remember.

Koran 24:32 And marry those among you who are single, or an honorable male or female slave. And if they are poor, then Allah will give them riches from His own bounty. Allah is bountiful and all-knowing.

Koran 4:25 If any of you is not wealthy enough to marry a free, believing woman, then allow him to marry a believing slave-girl. Allah knows your faith well, and you come from one another. Marry them with their master's permission, and give them a fair dowry, given that they are chaste, honorable, and have not had lovers. If the slave you marry commits adultery after you are married, then their punishment should be half of that commanded for a free woman. This is a law for those among you who fear sinning, but it will be better for you if you abstain. Allah is forgiving and merciful!

MOHAMMED AND THE SLAVE CODE

The examples of Mohammed's life form the basis of slave code.

[B3,46,695;B3,46,696;B2,18,163]
Mohammed ordered his followers to free slaves at the time of solar and lunar eclipses.

[B2,24,542;B2,24,543]
Mohammed said, "There is no tax on either a horse or a slave belonging to a Muslim"

[B2,25,579;B2,25,580;B2,25,587;B2,25,587]
Mohammed made it mandatory for every Muslim slave or free male or female – young or old – to pay a small tax, and he ordered that it be paid before the people went out to offer the 'Id prayer. [...]

Wala is the estate of the slave. When the slave dies their estate goes back to the one who freed them

[B3,34,378;B3,46,736;B8,80,749;B8,80,753;B8,80,748]

Mohammed, in forbidding the selling of the wala of slaves or giving it as a present, said: "The wala is for the liberator."

[B6,60,25;B8,80,732;B9,92,420;B9,83,44;B9,83,42;B9,83,42e]

Equality in punishment, called The Law of Retaliation was pre-scribed for Jews in the Bible, but the payment of blood money, was not ordained for them. Then, according to Mohammed, Allah de-clared that either blood money or equality in punishment (the free for the free, the slave for the slave, and the female for the female) is prescribed for Muslims in cases of murder.

[...]

[B3,34,362;B3,34,363;B3,46,731;B3,34,435]

Abu Huraira heard Mohammed saying, "If a slave-girl of yours commits illegal sexual intercourse and it is proved, she should be lashed, and after that nobody should blame her. If she commits illegal sexual intercourse the second time, she should be lashed and nobody should blame her after that. If she commits the offense for a third time and it is proved, she should be sold even for a hair rope."

[B9,86,100;B9,86,101]

Mohammed said, "A lady slave should not be given in marriage until she is consulted, and a virgin should not be given in marriage until her permission is granted." The people said, "How will she express her permission?" The Prophet said, "By keeping silent when asked her consent."

[...]

FREED SLAVES

Freed slaves run through the story of Islam. The *hima* is the common pasture of the Islamic state. At this time Umar is the caliph (ruler) and the hima is used for the livestock taken as a tax or taken in jihad. In order for this slave to be free, he had to become a Muslim.

[B4,52,292]

Umar appointed Hunai, his freed slave, to manage the hima. Umar told him, "Allow the shepherds with only a few camels or sheep to graze their animals, but do not allow livestock of the wealth to graze. If their livestock should perish, they have their farms and gardens to support them. But those who own only a few camels and sheep, if their livestock should perish, would bring their dependents to me and appeal for help. I could not ignore them and find it easier to let them have water and grass rather than to give them money from the Muslims' treasury."

The next hadith clearly identifies the freed slave as white. The race of a slave is always given, if the slave is not a Arab. Usually, the identified slave is black. This hadith also shows the moral structure of a Muslim oath. The question is, who determines whether the replacement for the oath is better? Conveniently, it the Muslim oath giver.

[B8,79,712]

Zahdam said: We were sitting with Abu Musa as we had ties of friendship and mutual favors between us. The meal was presented and there was chicken meat in it. Among those present was a white freed slave who did not eat. Abu Musa said to him, "Come along! I have seen Allah's Apostle eat chicken." The man said, "I have seen chickens eating something dirty, so I have taken an oath that I shall not eat them." Abu Musa said, "Listen, I will inform you about your oath:

"Once we went to Mohammed with a group of Ashairiyin, asking him for mounts while he was distributing some camels. Mohammed was in an angry mood at the time, and said 'By Allah! I will not give you mounts, and I have none.' After we had left, some camels of war treasure were brought to Allah's Apostle and he asked for us. We returned and he gave us five very fat good-looking camels. After we mounted them and went away, I said to my companions, Mohammed took an oath that he would not give us mounts, perhaps he forgot his oath. By Allah, we will never be successful, for we have taken advantage of the fact that Allah's Apostle forgot to fulfill his oath. So let us return and remind him.'

We returned and said, 'O Allah's Apostle! You took an oath that you would not give us mounts but later on you gave us mounts, and we thought that you have forgotten your oath.'

Mohammed said, 'Depart, for Allah has given you mounts. By Allah, Allah willing, if I take an oath and then later find another thing better than that, I do what is better, and make expiation for the oath.' "

A freed slave still is not fully free, but still has obligations to the master.

[B4,53,397;B8,80,747;B4,53,404;B3,30,94;B9,92,403]freedslavestillcontrolled

Ali delivered a sermon saying, "We have no book to recite except the Book of Allah and this written paper from the Prophet which contains legal verdicts regarding retaliation for wounds, the ages of the camels paid as tax or blood money, and the fact that Medina is a sanctuary. So, whoever commits heresy in it, or commits a sin or gives shelter to such a heretic in it will incur the Curse of Allah, the angels and all the people, and none of his compulsory or optional good deeds of worship will be accepted. And any freed slave who *sides with people other than those masters who freed him, without permission from the latter, will incur the Curse of Allah, the angels and all the people, and his compulsory and optional good deeds of worship will not be accepted." ...*

Wala is the estate that the slave accumulates. In short, Aisha, Mohammed's wife, would get whatever the slave had accumulated when the slave died. This is another example of how a freed slave is not as free as if they had never been enslaved. There is also a lesson in how many times a person is identified as a freed slave. It is a permanent attribute.

[B3,34,365:B3,46,737;B3,46,739;B8,79,708;B8,80,743;B7,65,341;B8,80,746;B8,8
0,750;B2,24,570;B3,47,752;B3,46,713;B3,46,735;B3,50,878;B3,50,889;B3,50,893-
;B8,80,751;B3,34,377;B3,34,364]

Aisha intended to buy the slave girl Barira in order to free her, but Barira's masters stipulated that after her death her wala would be for them. '

Aisha mentioned that to Mohammed who told her, "Buy her, as the wala is for the one who pays." He then called Barira and gave her the option of either staying with her husband or leaving him. Barira said she preferred her freedom to her husband...

[B3,46,707;B3,46,708]

When Abu Huraira and his slave set out intending to embrace Islam they lost each other on the way. Abu Huraira went to Mohammed and pledged allegiance to Islam. As he was sitting with Mohammed, his slave appeared and Mohammed said, "O Abu Huraira! Your slave has come back." Abu Huraira said, "Indeed, I would like you to witness that I free him for Allah's sake." Then he recited a poetic verse:- 'What a long, tedious, tiresome night! Nevertheless, it has delivered us from the land of disbelief.'

Here are two recollections of freed slaves. "Paradise is under the shade of swords" is the most poetic expression of jihad.

[B4,52,210;B4,52,266l]

Salim, Umar's freed slave and his clerk, said that Abdullah once wrote a letter to Umar. The letter said that Mohammed, in one of his military expeditions against the enemy, waited till the sun declined and then he got up amongst the people saying, "O people! Do not wish to meet the enemy, ask Allah for safety, and when you face the enemy, be patient and remember that Paradise is under the shades of swords."

Then he said, "O Allah, the Revealer of the Holy Book, and the Mover of the clouds and the Defeater of the clans, defeat them, and grant us victory over them."

[B8,75,342;B8,77,612]

Warrad, the freed slave of Al-Mughira, said that Muawiya wrote to Mughira. 'Write to me what you heard the Prophet saying at the end of every prayer after the Taslim.' So Al-Mughira dictated to me and said, "I heard the Prophet saying after the prayer, 'None has the right to be worshipped but Allah Alone Who has no partner. O Allah! No one can withhold what You give, and none can give what You withhold, and only good deeds are of value."

A GOOD SLAVE

A good slave is a Muslim and tries in every way to please his Muslim master.

[B3,46,723;B4,52,255:B4,55,655;B7,62,20]

Mohammed said, "Three persons will get a double reward:
A person who has a slave girl, educates her properly, teaches her good manners (without violence), then frees and marries her.
A man who believes in Jesus and then believes in me.
A slave who observes Allah's Rights and Obligations and is sincere to his master."

[B3,46,722;B3,46,726;B3,46,727]

Mohammed said, "If a slave is honest and faithful to his master and worships his Lord (Allah) in a perfect manner, he will get a double reward."

For a slave to flee his Islamic master is a sin against Allah.

M001,0131

Mohammed: "If a slave flees his master, Allah does not hear his prayer."

The next story comes from the Sira. Washi is a Kafir slave at the time of this battle. Washi was promised his freedom if he would kill Hamza, who had killed the owner's relative at an earlier battle. But after Mohammed had conquered Mecca, Washi had the good sense to submit to Islam. Hamza was Mohammed's uncle and only conversion saved his life.

Notice the reference to the Arabic custom of removing the clitoris of the Arab women.

I564 The slave Washi said, 'By God, I was looking at Hamza while he was killing men with his sword, sparing no one, when Siba came up to him before me, and Hamza said, "*Come here, you son of a female circumciser*," and he struck him a blow so swiftly that it seemed to miss his head. I poised my javelin until I was sure that it would hit the mark, and launched it at him. It pierced the lower part of his body and came out between his legs. He came on towards me, but collapsed and fell. I left him there until he died, when I came and recovered my javelin. Then I went off to the camp, for I had no business with anyone but him.'

EUNUCHS

Before Islam, the Arabs had the custom of castrating slaves. After Islam was established, the castration was done by the slave trader outside of Islam. Muslims paid more for a eunuch since it could be used in the harem.

> Koran 24:31 *And tell the women who are believers that they should lower their eyes and guard their purity, and they should not display their beauty and adornments except that which is normally shown. They should cover their breasts with their veils and only show their adornments to their husband, father-in-law, sons, step-sons, brothers, nephews, or their female servants, eunuch slaves, and children who are innocent and do not notice a woman's nakedness. And do not let them stamp their feet so as to reveal their hidden adornments [ankle bracelets]. Believers, all of you turn to Allah and repent so that it will go well for you.*

The man in this story was a slave. In all probability, he was black, since African men were castrated, not by removing the testicles, but the penis and testicles.

> M037, 6676
> *Anas reported that a person was charged with fornication with Mohammed's slave-girl. Mohammed said to Ali: Go and strike his neck. Ali came to him and he found him in a well making his body cool. Ali said to him: Come out, and as he took hold of his hand and brought him out, he found that his sexual organ had been cut. Ali refrained from striking his neck. He came to Mohammed and said: Allah's Messenger, he has not even the sexual organ with him.*

LANGUAGE

Islam has a very detailed language for a complete and sophisticated system of slavery.

abd, a slave, usually a black slave. Abd is also the word for any African or any black person.

abiq, a fugitive slave.

amah, a female slave.

ghilman, a male sex slave, usually a boy.

ghulam, a modern term for a slave.

ghurrah, a slave worth 500 dirhams.

ibaq, the freeing of slaves.

ibnu baydailjabin, the son of a mother with a white forehead [a free mother].

ibnu jurratin, the son of a free mother.

istilad, a legal term signifying that a Muslim master has freed a female slave who has born his child.

istibra, the waiting period for determining whether the slave is pregnant or not.

itaq, freeing a slave.

khaadim, a servant/slave.

kinn, a slave who is not mukatab, nor mudabbar, nor umm walad, nor mubaad, but entirely unfree.

kitaba, a form of a slave buying their freedom.

madhun lahu, a slave who can make business agreements for his master.

mamluk, a slave, usually a white slave.

ma malakat aimanukum, that which your right hand (the sword hand) possesses, a slave taken in jihad. Used in the Koran.

maula, a term used in Islamic law for a slave.

mubaad, a slave with several owners.

mudabbar, a slave who is freed on his master's death.

mukarkas, people having slaves mothers among their ancestors.

mukatab, slaves who ransom themselves from their master.

mustabad, slave.

mutaq, a freed slave.

mutiq, the master who frees a slave.

qinn, a slave born from slave parents.

raqabah, the term used for a captured slave.

raqiiq, slave.

surriyah, a Kafir woman slave used for sex. She may be bought, taken as a captive, or descended from a slave.

tadbir, a legal term for freeing a slave after the death of the master.

ubudiyah, slavery.

ummu al walad, a legal term for a slave who has borne the master's child.

umm walad, the enslaved mother married to a slave, who gives birth to his child.

wala, when freed slaves die, their estate goes to the one who freed them.

walau l ataqah, the relationship between a master and the freed slave.

zall, a fugitive child slave.

This is the Sunna of Mohammed

SEXUAL SLAVERY

CHAPTER 3

24:54 Say: Obey Allah and the Messenger.

- Having sex with your female slaves is a moral good.
- A married slave can be used for sex.
- The captives of jihad can be used for sex.
- Mohammed always got the pick of the captives to be used for sex.

For a Muslim to have sex with his slaves is in the same moral category as being humble, telling the truth or giving to charity. There is no blame and it is a moral good since it is allowed by the Koran. Allah only allows good. Sex with your slaves is only good for the male Muslim. Of course, for the female Muslim, it is a great sin.

There is a great advantage of having sex with slaves. None of the restrictions of sex apply to the slave, except for sex during the slave's menstrual period. Other than that, anything goes.

> Koran 23:1 *The successful ones will be the believers who are humble in their prayers who avoid vain conversation, who contribute to the needy, and who abstain from sex, except with their wives or slaves, in which case they are free from blame, but those who exceed these limits are sinners. Those who honor their promises and contracts and who pay strict attention to their prayers will inherit Paradise. They will dwell there forever.*

> Koran 70:22 *Not the devout, who pray constantly and whose wealth has a fixed portion set aside for beggars and the destitute, and those who believe in the Judgment Day, and those who fear their Lord's punishment—because no one is safe from their Lord's punishment—and who control their sexual desires, except with their wives or slave-girls, with them there is no blame; but whoever indulges their lust beyond this are transgressors), and who keep their trusts and promises, and who tell the truth, and who are attentive to their prayers. These will live with honors in Gardens.*

If the slave is married, then it is still morally good for a Muslim to have sex with her.

> 4:24 *Also forbidden to you are married women unless they are your slaves. This is the command of Allah. Other than those mentioned, all other women are lawful to you to court with your wealth and with honorable intentions, not with lust. And give those you have slept with a dowry, as it is your duty. But after you have fulfilled your duty, it is not an offense to make additional agreements among you. Truly Allah is knowing and wise!*

The above verse was given at the time of the jihad at Khaybar. Mohammed attacked the Jews of Khaybar and conquered them. The Jews that survived were doomed to become *dhimmis*. A dhimmi is not a Muslim, but one who has agreed to do all things as Islam wishes. In this case the surviving Jews were to work the land and give half of the proceeds to the jihadists. In addition, some women were taken as sex slaves. Mohammed, after taking the most beautiful Jew for his own pleasure, laid out the rules for sex with the captives.

- The marriage of the captive woman is annulled, as per the above Koran verse.
- Don't rape a pregnant slave. Wait until she has delivered.
- Don't have sex with a woman who is having her period.

> 1758 Dihya had asked Mohammed for Safiya, and when he chose her for himself Mohammed gave Safiya's two cousins to Dihya in exchange. *The women of Khaybar were distributed among the Muslims.*
>
> 1759 A man said, 'Let me tell you what I heard the apostle say on the day of Khaybar. He got up among us and said: "It is not lawful for a Muslim *to mingle his seed with another man's [meaning to have sex with a pregnant woman among the captives], nor is it lawful for him to take her until he has made sure that she is in a state of cleanness [not having her period].*

Here we see that at first the jihadists were reluctant to have sex with the captive women because of their husbands being nearby. But the Koran established that it was not immoral for them to rape Kafir women because they had husbands.

> M008, 3432
>
> *Mohammed sent an army to Autas and encountered the enemy and fought with them. Having overcome them and taken them captives, the Companions seemed to refrain from having intercourse with captive women because of their husbands being polytheists. Then Allah, Most High, sent down regarding that: "And women*

already married, except those whom your right hands possess (iv. 24)" (i. e. they were lawful for them when their menstral period came to an end).

JIHAD AND SEXUAL SLAVERY

The use of women for sex after jihad is a constant in the Hadith and the Sira. Here the men are asking about *coitus interruptus* to avoid pregnancy in the sex slaves. If they were pregnant, they had no value on the market as a sex slave. A Muslim is not supposed to have sex with a woman who is carrying another man's child, as per the Koran.

[B3,34,432;B7,62,137;B8,77,600]
Once some of Mohammed's soldiers asked if it was acceptable to use coitus interruptus to avoid impregnating the female captives they had received as their share of the booty.

Mohammed asked, "Do you really do that?" He repeated the question three times, then said: "It is better for you not to do it, for there is no soul which Allah has ordained to come into existence but will be created."

[B5,59,459:B3,46,718]
Ibn Muhairiza entered the Mosque and saw Abu Said and sat beside him and asked him about coitus interruptus. Abu Said said, "We went out with Allah's Apostle for jihad. We received captives and we desired women and celibacy became hard on us and we loved to do coitus interruptus. So when we intended to do coitus interruptus, we said, 'How can we do coitus interruptus before asking Allah's Apostle who is present among us?" We asked him about it and he said, 'It is better for you not to do so, for if any soul is predestined to exist, it will exist."

Mohammed instituted a temporary marriage of three days. Later this was canceled. However, the Shia Muslims still honor the temporary marriage.

[B6,60,139;B7,62,9;B7,62,130;]
Those who participated in the holy wars carried on by Mohammed had no wives throughout that time. They asked Mohammed, "Shall we castrate ourselves?" But he forbade them to do that and thereafter allowed them to marry women temporarily by giving them garments, and then he recited:

Koran 5:87 Oh, you who believe, do not forbid the good things that Allah allows you, but do not commit excess for Allah does not love those who commit excess.

Notice that Jadd assumes that the Muslims will be raping after they win the battle. That was the normal and expected behavior.

1894 One day when Mohammed was making his arrangements for the upcoming battle and said to Jadd: 'Would you like to fight the B. Asfar, Jadd?' He replied, 'Will you allow me to stay behind and not tempt me, for everyone knows that I am strongly addicted to women and I am afraid that if I see the Byzantine women I shall not be able to control myself.'

1689 When Saed reached Mohammed and the Muslims, the apostle told them to get up to greet their leader. Saed asked, 'Do you swear by Allah that you accept the judgment I pronounce on them?' They said 'Yes,' and he said, 'And is it incumbent on the one who is here?' looking in the direction of Mohammed, and Mohammed answered, 'Yes.' Saed said, 'Then I give judgment that the men should be killed, the property divided, and the women and children taken as captives.'

The Jewish women were later wholesaled by Mohammed to buy more horses and weapons for jihad.

If it were not for the cruelty of jihad, this next story has some humor. The female captive might bring a high ransom due to her high status. Mohammed said that he was going to return all of the captives at a price of six camels. Vyayna felt that she was worth more than that. His companions point out that she has no value for sex, she is not a virgin nor a plump matron.

1878 Vyayna took an old woman of Hawazin as a captive and said as he took her, 'I see that she is a person of standing in the tribe and her ransom may well be high.' When Mohammed returned the captives at a price of six camels each, Vyayna refused to give her back. Zuhayr told him to let her go, for her mouth was cold and her breasts flat; she could not conceive and her husband would not care and her milk was not rich. So he let her go for the six camels when Zuhayr said this. They allege that when Vyayna met al-Aqra later he complained to him about the matter and he said: By God, you didn't take her as a virgin in her prime nor even a plump middle-aged matron!'

Jihad can be ugly:

1980 When Zayd had raided the Fazara tribe, he and others were injured. Zayd swore he would never have sex until he had avenged his injuries. When he was well, Mohammed sent him against the Fazara.

26

He was successful and captured some of the women. One of them was an old woman, Umm Qirfa, whose husband he had killed. Zayd tied a rope to each leg of Umm Qirfa and tied each rope to a camel and pulled her apart. Her daughter was taken captive and passed around to three different men to use as they would for their pleasure.

MOHAMMED AND SEXUAL SLAVERY

Mohammed was so pure that he would not touch a Muslim woman's hand. But he would have sex with his slaves. This is an excellent example of ethical dualism. There is not one ethical code for all, but two ethical codes—one for the free Muslim and another for the slave.

[B9,89,321]

Mohammed used to take the Pledge of allegiance from the women by words only after reciting this verse: "...that they will not associate anything in worship with Allah." (60.12) And the hand of Allah's Apostle did not touch any woman's hand except the hand of that woman his right hand possessed. (i.e. his captives or his lady slaves).

Here we see that it was expected that the captive women would be used for sex. The jihadist's question about Mohammed is not whether he will have sex with Safiya, but as a wife or slave.

[B7,62,89;B5,59,524;B1,8,367]

[...]

We conquered Khaybar, took captives, and booty was collected.

Dihya asked Mohammed for one of the captive slave girls and was told he could go and take any one he wished. He took Safiya bint Huyai. Later Mohammed was told that Safiya was chief mistress of the tribes of Quraiza and An-Nadir and was suited for none but himself. So the Prophet called Dihya and Safiya to him and told Dihya that he could take any other slave girl but her. Mohammed then freed Safiya."

Mohammed stayed for three nights between Khaybar and Medina and was married to Safiya. Anas invited the Muslims to a banquet which included neither meat nor bread, but Mohammed ordered leather mats to be spread, on which dates, dried yogurt and butter were provided. The Muslims wondered whether Safiya would be considered as Mohammed's wife or as a slave. Then they said, "If the Prophet makes her observe the veil, then she will be one of his wives, but if he does not make her observe the veil, then she will be his slave." When Mohammed departed, he made a place for Safiya behind him on his camel and made her observe the veil.

27

Here is another situation in jihad where Mohammed got a new sexual partner.

> [B3,46,717]
>
> Ibn Aun wrote a letter to Nafi. Nafi wrote in reply that the Prophet had suddenly attacked Bani Mustaliq tribe without warning while they were heedless and their cattle were being watered at the places of water. Their fighting men were killed and their women and children were taken as captives; the Prophet got Juwairiya on that day.

The problem here is not that someone had sex with a slave, but that it was not her owner.

> [B3,34,421;B4,51,8;B8,80,757;B3,34,269;B9,89,293;B3,46,710;B3,41,603;B8,80,741]
>
> Saed and Abu quarreled over a boy born to the slave girl of Zama. They took the case of their claim of ownership to Mohammed. Saed said, "This (boy) is the son of my brother, Utba, and I promised to be his custodian." Abu bin Zama said, "O Allah's Apostle! This is my brother and was born on my father's bed from his slave-girl." Mohammed looked at the boy and saw a definite resemblance to Utba and then said, "The boy is yours, O Abu bin Zama. The child goes to the owner of the bed and the adulterer gets nothing but stones (despair, i.e. to be stoned to death). Then Mohammed said to his wife Sauda bint Zama, "Screen yourself from this boy," so Sauda never saw him again.

Mohammed's love for one of his slaves, Mary, caused an uproar in his harem. Mohammed was fond of a Coptic (Egyptian Christian) slave named Mary. Hafsa found Mohammed in her room with Mary, a violation of Hafsa's domain. He told a jealous Hafsa that he would stop relations with Mary and then did not. But Hafsa was supposed to be quiet about this matter. But the Koran points out to his wives and Muslims that he can have sex with his slaves as he wishes. Therefore, when he told Hafsa he would quit, he was not bound by that oath.

> Koran 66:1 Why, Oh, Messenger, do you forbid yourself that which Allah has made lawful to you? Do you seek to please your wives? Allah is lenient and merciful. Allah has allowed you release from your oaths, and Allah is your master. He is knowing and wise.

And last, but not least, after life is over, Muslims will still be having sex with slaves.

Hadith 101, Ibn Arabi, *Mishkat*

[...]

Allah says to the Muslims in Paradise: Go to your slave-girls and concubines in the garden of Paradise.

[...]

This is the Sunna of Mohammed

MOHAMMED AND SLAVERY

CHAPTER 4

*3:53 "Our Lord! We believe in what Thou hast
revealed, and we follow the Apostle; then write
us down among those who bear witness."*

- Mohammed was surrounded by slaves all of his life.
- Mohammed, the white man, owned many slaves, including black slaves.
- Slaves played a part in every aspect of Mohammed's life, including building his pulpit.
- Mohammed bought and sold slaves in both retail and wholesale lots.
- Sex slaves were part of Mohammed's harem.
- Mohammed gave slaves as gifts and received them as gifts.

Just as Mohammed is the model husband, he is also the model slave owner and slave trader. His Sunna shows the way for Muslims in all aspects of life. There was no aspect of slavery that Mohammed did not practice. Slavery was literally in the very milk he drank as a child.

[B7,64,285]
> One of Mohammed's wives, Um Habiba, said to him, "Will you marry my sister? I am not your only wife, and the person I'd like most to share the good with me, is my sister."
>
> Mohammed said, "That is not lawful for me." Um Habiba, "O Allah's Apostle! We have heard that you want to marry the daughter of Um Salama?"
>
> Mohammed said, "She is unlawful for me, for she is my foster niece. The freed slave girl Thuwaiba suckled both me and Abu Salama. You should not present your daughters and sisters to me for marriage."

His first wife, Khadija, owned a slave who plays a small part in Mohammed's role as a messenger of Allah. This story is one of several in the Sira which has Jews, Christians and soothsayers predicting the arrival of Mohammed.

I121 Khadija had a cousin, Waraqa, who was a Christian who had studied the scriptures and was a scholar. She told him what her slave, Maysara, had told her. The slave had been with Mohammed when a monk in Syria had seen two angels shading Mohammed. Waraqa said, 'If this is true, Khadija, verily Mohammed is the prophet of this people. I knew that a prophet of this people was to be expected. His time has come,' or words to that effect.

Mohammed used to sit and talk with a young Christian slave.

I261 Mohammed used often sat at the booth of a young Christian called Jabr, a slave. The Meccans used to say *'The one who teaches Mohammed most of what he brings is Jabr, the Christian slave.'* Then Allah revealed in reference to their words, "We well know that they say, 'Only a mortal teaches him.' The tongue of him at whom they hint is foreign, and this is a clear Arabic tongue."

SLAVES IN MOHAMMED'S HOME

Here we have a Koranic reference to Mohammed's slaves in his home.

33:55 *There is no blame on the Messenger's wives if they speak unveiled with their fathers, sons, brothers, nephews on either their brother's or sister's side, their women, or their slave-girls. Women! Fear Allah, for Allah witnesses all things.*

[B9,92,462]
Aisha said that the Divine Inspiration was delayed after the slanderers gave a false statement against her, so Mohammed called upon Ali and Osama to consult with them about the question of divorcing her. Osama said what he knew about Aisha's innocence, but Ali pointed out Allah had not put restrictions on Mohammed and that there were many women other than her. He suggested asking the slave girl because she would tell the truth."

So Mohammed asked Aisha's slave girl, Barira, if she had seen anything that aroused her suspicion. ...

Barira was the slave girl of Aisha, Mohammed's wife.

[B7,63,204;B7,63,205]
Ibn Abbas: said that Barira's husband was Mughith – the black slave of Bani so-and-so—and used to walk behind her along the streets of Medina.

It is intriguing how the race of a slave is frequently given. Mohammed had more than one black slave.

[B7,72,734:]

[...]

He said, 'Greater than that! Allah's Apostle has divorced his wives! I went to them and found all of them weeping in their dwellings, and the Prophet had ascended to an upper room of his. At the door of the room there was his black slave to whom I went and said, 'Ask the permission for me to enter.' He admitted me and I entered to see the Prophet lying on a mat.

[...]

[B8,73,182;B8,73,221]

Once Um Sulaym was on a journey with Mohammed and Mohammed's black slave Anjasha, who was driving the camels very fast. The women in charge of the luggage were riding on those camels, and Mohammed said: "May Allah be merciful to you, O Anjasha! Drive the camels with the glass vessels (women) slowly!"

[B2,24,569]

Mohammed saw a dead sheep which had been given in charity to a freed slave-girl of Maimuna, the wife of Mohammed. Mohammed said, "Why don't you get the benefit of its hide?" They said, "It is dead." He replied, "Only to eat its meat is illegal."

Mohammed allows Aisha to watch some black slaves in the Mosque:

B2,15,103

During the days of Mina, Abu Bakr visited Aisha. While Mohammed was lying down, two young slave girls were beating a tambourine. Abu Bakr yelled at them to stop their noise. Mohammed uncovered his face and told Abu Bakr, "Leave them alone. It is a festival day."

Aisha also said, "One time Mohammed was hiding me from public view so that I might watch some black slaves in the Mosque display their skill with weapons.

Umar scolded them for exhibiting themselves in the presence of a Muslim woman, but Mohammed said, "Leave them alone. You Negroes may continue; you have my protection."

When men kill a slave shepherd of Mohammed's, they reap a terrible death.

I999 *Mohammed captured a slave called Yasar,* and he put him in charge of his milch-camels. Some men of Qays came to the apostle suffering with an illness, and the apostle told them that if they went to the milch-camels and drank their milk and urine they would recover. When they recovered their health, they fell upon the apostle's shepherd Yasar and killed him and stuck thorns in his eyes and drove away his camels. Mohammed sent Kurz in pursuit and he overtook them and brought them to the apostle as he returned from a jihad raid. Mohammed cut off their hands and feet and gouged out their eyes. They were left to die of thirst lying on sharp rocks. [Their wounds were cauterized so they did not bleed to death, but died of thirst.]

A Muslim accumulates merit by freeing slaves. Aisha was Mohammed's wife and she gets some easy merit here.

1983 The apostle sent him to raid them, and he killed some and captured others. Asim told me that Aisha said to *Mohammed that she must free a slave*, and he said, 'The captives are coming now. We will give you one whom you can set free.'

Mohammed also freed slaves.

1763 Abdullah told me from one of his family from Abu Rafi, *freed slave of Mohammed*: We went with Ali, Mohammed's nephew, when the apostle sent him into battle. When he got near the fort, the garrison came out and he fought them. A Jew struck him so that his shield fell from his hand, so Ali laid hold of a door by the fort and used it as a shield. He kept it in his hand as he fought until Allah gave victory, throwing it away when all was over.

Fatima was Mohammed's daughter.

[B5,57,55]
Fatima complained of the suffering caused to her by the hand mill. Some female slaves were brought to Mohammed, she came to him but did not find him at home. Aisha was there to whom Fatima told of her desire for a slave. When Mohammed came, Aisha informed him about Fatima's visit.

Slaves were part of Mohammed's funeral.

I1020 When the preparations for burial had been completed on the Tuesday, he was laid upon his bed in his house. Abu Bakr said, 'I heard the apostle say, "No prophet dies but he is buried where he died."' The bed on which he died was taken up and they made a grave beneath it. Then the people came to visit the apostle praying over him by companies: first came the men, then the women, then the children, *then the slaves.*

MOHAMMED AND THE TRADES

The pulpit that Mohammed spoke from was built by a slave.

[B1,8,374;B1,8,440;B2,13,40;B3,34,307;B3,34,308;B3,47,743]

Sahl bin Saed was asked about Mohammed's pulpit. He said Mohammed had sent for an Ansari woman who had a slave carpenter and asked to have a place built for him to sit when addressing the people. The slave gathered wood from the tamarisk and built the pulpit. Then Mohammed prayed on it, stepped down and prostrated himself on the ground at its foot, then ascended again and finished praying. Then Mohammed said: "I have done this so that you may follow me and learn the way I pray."

Mohammed had a slave tailor.

[B7,65,346;B7,65,344]

Anas said that when he was a young boy he once went walking with Mohammed. Mohammed entered the house of his slave tailor and was offered a dish of food covered with pieces of gourd, which he started eating. Anas said that he has loved to eat gourd since he saw Mohammed eating it.

Mohammed was medically treated by a slave. Cupping is an old medical treatment for bleeding, which supposedly had beneficial benefits.

[B3,34,412;B3,36,481;B3,34,315]

Mohammed sent for a slave who had the profession of cupping, and he cupped him. Mohammed ordered that the slave be paid a small amount and appealed to the slave's masters to reduce his taxes.

Mohammed ate food prepared by a slave.

[B3,43,636:B3,34,295;B7,65,345;B7,65,371]

An Ansari man called Abu Shuaib said to his slave butcher, "Prepare a meal sufficient for five persons so that I might invite Mohammed and four other persons." Abu Shuaib had seen signs of hunger on Mohammed's face. Another man, who was not invited, followed Mohammed, who said to Abu Shuaib, "This man has followed us. Do you allow him to share the meal?" Abu Shuaib said, "Yes, he is welcome." ...

MOHAMMED AND THE SALE OF SLAVES

[B3,34,351;B9,89,296;B3,34,351;B8,79,707;B9,85,80]achristianslave

Mohammed found out one of his companions had promised to free his slave after his death. Later on the man was in need of money, but he had no property other than that slave, so Mohammed took the slave and said, "Who will buy this slave from me?" Noaim

bin Abdullah bought the slave and Mohammed took its price and gave it to the owner.

Here Mohammed wholesales female slaves to fund jihad.

1693 Then Mohammed sent Saed with some of the captive Jewish women of B. Qurayza to Najd and he sold them for horses and weapons.

Mohammed was very parsimonious about all household expenses.

[B4,53,344;B7,64,274]
Fatima went to Mohammed to complain about the bad effect on her hand of grinding with the stone hand-mill. She heard that he had received the booty of a few slave girls and went to request one for a maidservant. Mohammed was not home, so she mentioned her problem to Aisha. When Mohammed returned, Aisha informed him about that. Later Ali said, "So the Prophet came to us when we had gone to bed. We wanted to get up but he said, 'Stay where you are.' Then he came and sat between me and Fatima, and I felt the coldness of his feet on my abdomen. He said, 'Shall I direct you to something better than what you have requested? When you go to bed say 'Glorified be Allah' thirty-three times, All the Praises are for Allah' thirty three times, and Allah is Great' thirty four times, for that is better for you than a servant.'"

MOHAMMED, SLAVES AND SEX

Mohammed got this sex slave from the Jews after he killed all of the adult males.

1693 Mohammed had chosen one of their women for himself, Ayhama, one of the women of Qurayza Jews, and she remained with him until she died, in his power. The apostle had proposed to marry her and put the veil on her, but she said: 'No, Leave me in your power, for that will be easier for me and for you.' So he left her. She had shown repugnance towards Islam when she was captured and clung to Judaism.

Here we have Koranic references to Mohammed's sex life and how it included sex slaves.

Koran 33:50 *Messenger! We allow you your wives whose dowries you have paid, and the slave-girls Allah has granted you as spoils of war, and the daughters of your paternal and maternal uncles and aunts who fled with you to Medina, and any believing woman who gives herself to the Messenger, if the Messenger wishes to marry her. This is a privilege for you only, not for any other believer. We know what We have commanded the believ-*

*ers concerning wives and slave-girls. We give you this privilege so you will
be free from blame. Allah is forgiving and merciful!*

*33:51 You may turn away any of them that you please, and take to your
bed whomever you please, and you will not be blamed for desiring one you
had previously set aside for a time. Therefore, it will be easier for you to
comfort them and prevent their grief and to be content with what you give
each of them. Allah knows what is in your hearts, and Allah is all-knowing
and gracious.*

*33:52 It will be unlawful for you to marry more wives after this or to ex-
change them for other wives, even though you are attracted by their beauty,
except slave-girls you own. [Mohammed had nine wives and several slave-
girls.] And Allah watches over all things.*

Here Mohammed gets a gift of four Christian slaves.

T1561,I972 Then Mohammed divided his companions and sent Salit
to the ruler... He handed over to him the apostle's letter and the ruler
gave Mohammed four slave girls, one of whom was Mary, mother of
Ibrahim the apostle's son.

Mohammed would not touch a female Muslim, but he would touch his
female slaves.

[B9,89,321]
Narrated Aisha:
*The Prophet used to take the Pledge of allegiance from the wom-
en by words only after reciting this Holy Verse:*

60:12 Oh, Messenger, when believing women come to you and
pledge an oath of allegiance to you and ascribe no other gods as
partners to Allah

*And the hand of Allah's Apostle did not touch any woman's
hand except the hand of that woman his right hand possessed. (i.e.
his captives or his lady slaves).*

Mohammed killed Safiya's husband, father and cousin, as well as many
members of her Jewish tribe. She choose to be his wife rather that his slave.

[B5,59,524]
*Mohammed stayed for three nights between Khaybar and Me-
dina and was married to Safiya. He invited the Muslims to his
marriage banquet and there was neither meat nor bread in that
banquet. Mohammed ordered Bilal to spread the leather mats on
which dates, dried yogurt and butter were put.*
*The Muslims said amongst themselves, "Will Safiya be one of
the wives of the Prophet or just a slave-girl?" Some of them said, "If*

*the Prophet makes her observe the veil, then she will be one of the
Prophet's wives, and if he does not make her observe the veil, then
she will be his slave-girl." So when he departed, he made a place for
her behind him on his camel and made her observe the veil.*

Mohammed made the same deal with Juwairiya.

[B3,46,717]

*Ibn Aun wrote a letter to Nafi and Nafi wrote in reply to my
letter that Mohammed had suddenly attacked the Bani Mustaliq
without warning while they were heedless and their cattle were being watered at the places of water. Their fighting men were killed
and their women and children were taken as slaves; the Prophet got
Juwairiya on that day.*

THE BEATING OF SLAVES

Mohammed stood by and prayed while his men beat and tortured two
slaves. He then took part in their interrogation.

I436 Then the apostle returned to his companions; and when night
fell he sent Ali, al-Zubayr and Saed, with a number of his companions
to the well at Badr in quest of news of both parties. They fell in with
some water-camels of the Quraysh, among whom were two slaves, and
they brought them along and questioned them while the apostle was
standing praying. They said, 'We are the water carriers of the Quraysh;
they sent us to get them water. 'The people were displeased, at their report, for they had hoped that they would belong to Abu Sufyan, so *they
beat the slaves, and when they had beaten them until they were weak,*
the two slaves said, 'We belong to Abu Sufyan,' so they let them go.

I436 The apostle bowed and prostrated himself twice, and said,
'When they told you the truth you beat them; and when they lied you
let them alone. They told the truth; they do belong to the Quraysh.

Mohammed stood by while one of his men beats a slave. This slave
lived in his house and was his favorite wife's slave.

I735 As for Ali he said: "Women are plentiful, and you can easily
change one for another. *Ask the slave girl,* for she will tell you the truth."
So Mohammed called Burayra to ask her, and Ali got up and *gave her a
violent beating, saying,* "Tell the apostle the truth," to which she replied,
"I know only good of her. The only fault I have to find with Aisha is
that when I am kneading dough and tell her to watch it she neglects it
and falls asleep and her pet lamb comes and eats it!"

Here Mohammed gives one of his men a fine home and a sex slave.

> 1739 Then they came to Mohammed and told him of the affair and he summoned Hassan and Safwan. The latter said, 'He insulted me and I became so angry I hit him.' Mohammed said to Hassan, 'Do you look with an evil eye on my people because Allah has guided them to Islam?' He added, 'Be charitable about what has befallen you.' Hassan said, 'It is yours.'
>
> 1739 To compensate him, Mohammed gave him a castle in Medina. *He also gave him Sirin, a Coptic (Egyptian Christian) slave girl, and she bore him a boy.* "

Mohammed was a generous man. Here he gives his foster sister two slaves:

> 1857 Yazid told me that when she was brought to the apostle she claimed to be his foster-sister, and when he asked for proof she said, 'The bite you gave me in my back when I carried you at my hip.' The apostle acknowledged the proof and stretched out his robe for her to sit on and treated her kindly. He gave her the choice of living with him in affection and honor or going back to her people with presents, and she chose the latter. The B. Saed allege that *Mohammed gave her a slave called Makhul and a slave girl*; the one married the other and their progeny still exist.

Here Mohammed receives a slave as a gift.

> 1963 Rifa'a came to the apostle during the armistice of al-Hudaybiya before Khaybar. *He gave the apostle a slave and he became a good Muslim.* The apostle gave him a letter to his people.

Mohammed gave sex slaves to his chief lieutenants. Umar, in turn, gave his sex slave to his son.

> 1878 Mohammed gave Ali a girl called Rayta and he gave Uthman a girl called Zaynab and he gave Umar a girl, whom Umar gave to his son Abdullah.

MOHAMMED'S WHITENESS

There is an odd item about race that must be mentioned. In America the descendants of slavery are told that Christianity is the white man's religion. Islam is the natural religion of the black man.

It is a fact that Islam is based upon the Sunna of Mohammed. The Sunna is exceedingly clear about race and Mohammed. The Hadith goes out of its way to say that Mohammed was white. So a white man who owned black slaves started the natural religion of the black man.

These are a few of the hadiths that report Mohammed's whiteness.

B4,56,765

When Mohammed prostrated himself to pray, he would spread his arms so wide apart, that we could see his armpits. Ibn Bukair described it as "the whiteness of his armpits."

B3,47,769

Mohammed delegated a man from the Al-Azd tribe to be a tax collector. When the man returned he said to Mohammed, "This is the money that I have collected for you and this money was given to me as a present."

Mohammed said, "If this man wanted presents, why didn't he stay at home with his parents? By Allah, if someone takes something from the tax collection, they will carry that weight around their neck on Judgment Day. If it is a camel, it will be grunting when he is judged; if it is a cow, it will be mooing; if it is a sheep it will be bleating."

Mohammed then raised his hands up high, exposing his white armpits, and said, "Allah, haven't I told the people your instructions?"

[B4,52,90;B490,769]

At the battle of Al-Ahzab I saw Mohammed carrying dirt which covered his white belly. He was saying, "Without your help Allah, we would have no guidance, we would neither pray nor give charitably. Give us peace and courage when we battle our enemies. Our enemies have rejected you and Mohammed, but we will never give up if they try to attack us."

B2,17,122

Abdullah Bin Dinar once heard Ibn Umar recite some of Abu Talib's poetic verse: "And a white man (Mohammed) who is asked to pray for rain and who is the protector of orphans and the guardian of widows."

B1,3,63

We were sitting with Mohammed in the Mosque one day when a man rode up on a camel. He asked, "Which one of you is Mohammed?" We answered, "That white man leaning on his arm..."

B1,8,367

Just before the battle of Khaybar, we and Mohammed gave the Fajr prayer before sunup. I [Anas] was riding behind Abu Talha and next to Mohammed. We were so close, that as we rode down the main street of Khaybar, my knee touched Mohammed's leg. His garment moved and exposed the whiteness of his thigh.

M004,1208

'Amir b. Sa'd reported: I saw the Messenger of Allah pronouncing taslim on his right and on his left till I saw the whiteness of his cheek.

M030,5778:

Abu Tufail reported: I saw Allah's Messenger and there is one amongst the people of the earth who are living at the present time and had seen him except me. I said to him: How did you find him? He said: He had an elegant white color, and he was of an average height.

OTHER REMARKS ABOUT RACE

Mohammed's Night Journey is known by every Muslim. The house he stayed in that night had a black slave.

1267 Um Hani said: 'The apostle went on no night journey except while he was in my house. He slept that night in my house. He prayed the final night prayer, then he slept and we slept. A little before dawn the apostle woke us, and when we had prayed the dawn prayer he said, "Umm Hani', I prayed with you the last evening prayer in this valley as you saw. Then I went to Jerusalem and prayed there. Then I have just prayed the morning prayer with you as you see." He got up to go out and I took hold of his robe. I said, "O prophet of Allah, don't talk to the people about it for they will give you the lie and insult you." He said, "By Allah, I certainly will tell them." *I said to a Negress, a slave of mine,* "Follow the apostle and listen to what he says to the people, and what they say to him."

1357 Mohammed said, 'Whoever wants to see Satan should look at Nabtal!' He was a black man with long flowing hair, inflamed eyes, and dark ruddy cheeks.... Allah sent down concerning him:

9:61 *To those who annoy the Prophet there is a painful doom.*

1357 Gabriel came to Mohammed and said, 'If a black man comes to you, his heart is more gross than a donkey's.'

B9,89,256

Mohammed said, 'You should listen to and obey your ruler even if he is a black slave whose head looks like a raisin.'

1614 Thabit said, "It is your folly to fight the Apostle, for Allah's army is bound to disgrace you. We brought them to the pit. Hell was their meeting place. We collected them there, black slaves, men of no descent."

1562 The black troops and slaves of the Meccans cried out and the Muslims replied, 'Allah destroy your sight, you impious rascals.'

B4,52,137

Mohammed said, 'Let the black slave of Dinar perish. And if he is pierced with a thorn, let him not find anyone to take it out for him.... If the black slave asks for anything it shall not be granted, and if he needs intercession to get into paradise, his intercession will be denied.'

This is the Sunna of Mohammed

THE HISTORY OF ISLAMIC SLAVERY

If you live in America, you know the modern historical theory of slavery. Evil white men brought Africans to the Western hemisphere, where they were sold for profit and put to work as slaves. The modern theory is true as far as it goes, but it does not go nearly far enough. Slavery goes far beyond the 300-year period when whites bought slaves from the Muslim wholesalers on the West coast of Africa.

Every culture has had some form of slavery in its past. Slavery is an answer to how to get hard, rough work done. We feel ethically superior to our ancestors because we don't have slaves. But the reason that slavery was finally ended was a combination of ethics and the discovery of a better slave—the machine.

WHITE SLAVES

For 1400 years—until the slave market was officially closed in the early 1960s—the highest priced slave in Mecca was the white woman. The price of a white slave girl was from three to ten times that of a black girl. When Islam invaded Spain, the first thing exported back to Islamic North Africa were a thousand blond-haired girls.

Our word for slave comes from the Slavs of eastern Europe. So many of them were taken by the Muslims of the Ottoman Empire that the very term *Slav* came to mean slave. Black slaves were so numerous that the term *abd* came to mean black or African. Muslims called the white slaves *mamluk*.

Not only were there words for slaves to differentiate them but the uses of the slaves were different. The white woman was favored for sex. That is why she brought the best price. White slaves were not used for rough labor but were used for higher positions in domestic and administrative work. Both white and black men were used as eunuchs in the harem.

Also both white and black male slaves were used in the armies of Islam; however, whites could become officers, governors, and rulers. Advancement happened only rarely for blacks. Only one black slave rose to the rank of ruler, Abu I Misk Kafur who was a eunuch and became a governor of Egypt.

In Eastern Europe, the Islamic rulers taxed the Christian families at the rate of one fifth; one child in five was taken for slavery. These children were forcibly converted to Islam and trained to form the core of the *janissaries*, the military troops used by the Turkish sultan. The sultan reserved younger children for the palace, where they were trained by the eunuchs for positions in the administration of the Islamic empire. This theft took place annually among the Greeks, Serbs, Bulgarians, Albanians, and Armenians. At a fixed date, each father had to appear in the town square for the sultan's man to come pick the best of his children for Islam.

The strategy ensured that the population of Muslims increased and the population of Christians decreased.

When the Serbs revolted against Islamic oppression and were crushed in 1813, eighteen hundred women and children were sold in one day to Muslims in Belgrade.[1] During the Greek revolt against Islamic rule, the Islamic ruler sent four to five thousand rebels to be sold in Constantinople and thirty-four hundred women to be sold as slaves.[2]

In the seventeenth century, Jean de Chardin wrote:

> Shah Abbas I transported settlements of twenty or thirty thousand souls at a time, two or three hundred leagues from their native land. Almost all of them were Georgian and Armenian Christians [...] It was in this way that the kings of Persia rose to that point of absolute power which I will show, and which they sustain [...] because as almost all the Georgians and Iberians [from South Caucasus region] who are given the status to govern are slaves by origin, and genuine outsiders in the government, they have no contacts either in the kingdom or with one another. As most of them know neither from where nor from whom they come, it happens that they are not driven by any desire for freedom on the one hand and are incapable of forming leagues or conspiracies on the other. Men who have no relationship among themselves do not rise in rebellion on behalf of each other, either to save their lives or to ascend the throne.
>
> This name of *coular* means slave, not that these men are not as free as other Persians, but because they are natives of countries such as Georgia, Circassia, Iberia, and of Moscow, from where slaves are drawn. Thus they are of Christian origin. Some were sent to the king as gifts, being still young; others are descended from the peoples of these countries,

---

1. Castellan, *Histoire des Balkans*, 254.
2. Broughton, *Travels,* letter written May 11, 1825 by Jean-Bafriel Eynard.

who have become accustomed to Persia. As almost all of them embrace the Islamic religion, they are all renegades or the children of renegades.[3]

BLACK SLAVES

In theory, the races are equal in Islam, but they have not been so in practice. Long before Islam, the Arabs had enslaved blacks. After Islamic expansion, the Islamic empire needed more slaves, so they came from the traditional source, sub-Saharan Africa. Massive importation of illiterate people performing hard labor did not enhance the Muslim view of blacks, no matter how vital they had been in Mohammed's day. Here is one caliph's opinion of the black slave he received as a gift:

> Had you been able to find a smaller number than one and a worse color than black you would have sent that as a gift.[4]

And another opinion:

> Therefore, the Negro nations are, as a rule, submissive to slavery because Negroes have little that is essentially human and have attributes that are quite similar to those of dumb animals, as we have stated.[5]

The major exploitation of black slaves took place outside the cities. Since Islam is primarily an urban culture, it is the urban culture recorded in its writings. Therefore, we don't know much about the lives of the rural slaves. The picture we have of Islamic slavery is that of the palace, the army, and domestic workers.

Large gangs of slaves were used for heavy construction, agriculture, mining, and dredging operations. Large landowners would employ thousands of black slaves for agricultural work. Urban slaves performing administrative and domestic work had relatively light duty, but those performing manual labor led a brutal life. The slaves, mainly men, who worked the Saharan salt mines lasted an average of five years before death. Slave women were used as prostitutes, although the practice was forbidden by the Koran. The Koran also says that if they are prostituted, Allah is forgiving.

Over time, there has been a great deal of discussion about the enslavement of Muslim blacks. Islamic law about this is exceedingly clear; any Kafir could be enslaved after jihad, but no Muslim, black or any

---

3. Jean de Chardin, *Voyages du Chevalier de Chardin En Perse*, Paris, 1811, 5226-28, 306-8.

4. Jahsihari, *Kitab Al-Wuzara wa l-Kuttab* (Cairo, 1938), p. 81.

5. Translated by F. Rosenthal, Ibn Khaldun, *The Muqaddimah*, vol. 1 (New York, 1958), p. 301.

other, was to be enslaved. To resolve the matter, one simply disputed the devoutness of the slave's faith and concluded he or she was "not really a Muslim."

The Muslims of North Africa captured so many of their black brothers that there was a body of legal rulings, *fatwas*, on the subject. The fatwas concluded that the benefit of the doubt went to the owner, not the slave.[6] There was an immediate outcry from black Muslim rulers, decrying the jihad launched against their subjects, and their black jurists protested the enslavement of Muslims, but the practice continued.[7]

Enslavement went hand in hand with death. Not only were family members killed protecting their loved ones, but many others died on the relentless march from their villages of capture. Only the best humans were taken; thus, villages were left under-populated with the young, weak, sick, and very old. Starvation, disease, and heartbreak destroyed those who remained. One author of the nineteenth century estimated that, for every slave on the auction block, nine others died.[8]

Here is a quote from David Livingstone about the aftermath of slave trading in Africa:

> Now as the exploring party ascended the river the desolation was heart-breaking. Corpses floated past them in such numbers that the paddle-wheels had to be cleared from them every morning. Wherever we took a walk, human skeletons were seen in every direction, and it was painfully interesting to observe the different postures in which the poor wretches had breathed their last. Many had ended their misery under shady trees, others under projecting crags in the hills, while others lay in their huts with closed doors, which when opened disclosed the moldering corpse with the poor rags around the loins, the skull fallen off the pillow, the little skeleton of the child, that had perished first, rolled up in a mat between two large skeletons. The sight of this desert, but eighteen months ago a well peopled valley, now literally strewn with human bones, forced the conviction upon us that the destruction of human life in the middle passage, however great, constitutes but a small portion of the waste, and made us feel that unless the slave-trade—that monster inequity, which has so long brooded over Africa—is put down, awful commerce cannot be established.[9]

---

6. Amad Al-Wansharisi, *Kitab Al-Miyar Al-mughrib*, vol. 9 (1895-96), 71-72

7. EII, s.v. "Abd" (by r. Brunschvig), p.32a; Rotter, *Die Stellung des Negers*, 44, 49ff.

8. Hourst, *Mission hydorgraphique du Niger*, 1896.

9. Mrs. J. H. Worcester, Jr., *Life of David Livingstone* (Chicago: Women's Presbyterian Board of Missions of the Northwest, 1888), 59-60.

And why did the killing and slaving take place?

> We had a long discussion about the slave trade. The Arabs have told the chief that "our object in capturing slaves is to get them into our own possession and make them of our own religion."[10]

And what was the emotional impact on the survivors?

> The strangest disease I have seen in this country seems really to be broken-heartedness, and it attacks non-Muslim men who have been captured and made slaves. Speaking with many who died from it, they ascribed their only pain to the heart, and placed the hand correctly on the spot, though many think that the organ stands high up under the breast-bone. Some slavers expressed surprise to me that they should die, seeing they had plenty to eat and no work. It seems to be really broken hearts of which they die.[11]

Islamic slavery was the basis of all the slavery in the West. When the white slaver arrived in his boat on the coast of Africa, he went to see a Muslim trader. The New World was a new market for the ancient Islamic slave trade. The only change was the boat and the direction it sailed. Three hundred years went by before the Atlantic slave trade was stopped. But it never has stopped in Islam.

AFRICAN DEATHS DUE TO SLAVERY

Thomas Sowell estimates that 11 million slaves were shipped across the Atlantic and 14 million were sent to the Islamic nations of North Africa and the Middle East[12]. For every slave captured many others died. Estimates of this collateral damage vary. The renowned missionary David Livingstone estimated that for every slave who reached the plantation five others died by being killed in the raid or died on the forced march from illness and privation[13]. Those who were left behind were the very young, the weak, the sick and the old. These soon died since the main providers had been killed or enslaved. So, for 25 million slaves delivered to the market, we have the death of about 120 million people due to the Islamic wholesale slave trade in Africa over the centuries.

---

10. Ibid. 62.
11. Ibid.
12. Thomas Sowell, *Race and Culture*, BasicBooks, 1994, p. 188.
13. Woman's Presbyterian Board of Missions, *David Livingstone*, p. 62, 1888.

SEX SLAVES

The great Islamic geographer, Al-Idris, was of the opinion that Nubian women made the best slaves of pleasure.

> Their women are of surpassing beauty. They are circumcised and fragrant-smelling...their lips are thin, their mouths small and their hair flowing. Of all black women, they are the best for the pleasures of the bed...It is on account of these qualities of theirs that the rulers of Egypt were so desirous of them and outbid others to purchase them, afterwards fathering children from them.[14]

By the early nineteenth century the taste in slaves for sex (concubines) had changed to Ethiopian women, at least in Mecca.

> There are few families at Mecca, in moderate circumstances, that do not keep slaves...the concubines are always Abyssinian slaves. Wealthy Meccans do not prefer domestic peace over the gratification of their passions; they keep mistresses in common with their lawful wives...Many Meccans have no other than Abyssinian wives, finding the Arabians more expensive, and less disposed to yield to the will of the husband...The same practice is adopted by many foreigners, who reside in the Hijaz for a short time. Upon their arrival, they buy a female companion, with the design of selling her at their departure; but sometimes their stay is protracted; the slave bears a child; they marry her, and become stationary in the town. There are very few unmarried men, or those without a slave.[15]

When wealthy Muslims had enough money, they preferred white sex slaves. A white female slave was about three times more expensive than an Ethiopian woman.

> The white female slaves are mostly in the possession of wealthy Turks. The concubine slaves in the houses of Egyptians of the higher and middle classes are, generally, what are termed "Habasheeyehs," that is, Abyssinians.[16]

There is one more aspect of sexual slavery involving mutilation: the eunuchs. The removal of a man's sex organs made him socially available to all women, even in the harem. Since Islamic prohibitions would not

---

14.   J. O. Hunwick, "Black Africans in the Islamic World: An Understudied, Dimension of the Black Diaspora," *Tarikh 5* (1978), no. 4:27.

15.   John Lewis Burckhardt, *Travels in Arabia, vol. 1* (London:1829), 340-42.

16.   E. W. Lane, *An Account of the Manners and Customs of the Modern Egyptians,* 5th ed., vol. 1 (London: 1871), 168-169, 233-34.

allow Muslims to castrate slaves, they chose to pay a higher price for slaves castrated in *dar al harb*, [outside of Islamic territory] not *dar al Islam*.

There is a fascinating aspect of Islamic castration: white male slaves had only their testicles removed. Blacks lost both testicles and penis. Black eunuchs were traditionally used for the attendants of the Mosque of the Prophet in Medina.

HINDU SLAVERY

If you study the history of slavery there is no mention of the existence of massive slavery in India. As always, the slavery was the result of jihad.

Koenard Elst in *Negationism in India*[17] gives an estimate of 80 million Hindus killed in the total jihad against India. The country of India today is only half the size of ancient India, due to jihad. The mountains near India are called the Hindu Kush, meaning the "funeral pyre of the Hindus".

Here is just one small part of the killing of 80,000,000 Hindus and the taking of slaves:

> When Mahmud Ghaznavi attacked Waihind in 1001-02, he took 500,000 persons of both sexes as captives. This figure of Abu Nasr Muhammad Utbi, the secretary and chronicler of Mahmud, is so mind-boggling that Elliot reduces it to 5000. The point to note is that taking of slaves was a matter of routine in every expedition. Only when the numbers were exceptionally large did they receive the notice of the chroniclers. So that in Mahmud's attack on Ninduna in the Punjab (1014), Utbi says that "slaves were so plentiful that they became very cheap; and men of respectability in their native land (India) were degraded by becoming slaves of common shop-keepers (in Ghazni)". His statement finds confirmation in later chronicles including Nizamuddin Ahmad's Tabqat-i-Akbari which states that Mahmud "obtained great spoils and a large number of slaves". Next year from Thanesar, according to Farishtah, "the Muhammadan army brought to Ghaznin 200,000 captives so that the capital appeared like an Indian city, for every soldier of the army had several slaves and slave girls". Thereafter slaves were taken in Baran, Mahaban, Mathura, Kanauj, Asni etc. When Mahmud returned to Ghazni in 1019, the booty was found to consist of (besides huge wealth) 53,000 captives. Utbi says that "the number of prisoners may be conceived from the fact that, each was sold for from two to ten dirhams. These were afterwards taken to Ghazna, and the merchants came from different cities to purchase them, so that the countries of Mawarau-un-Nahr, Iraq and Khurasan (Persia) were filled with them".

---

17.   Koenard Elst, *Negationism in India*, Voice of India, New Delhi, 2002, pg. 34.

The Tarikh-i-Alfi adds that the fifth share due to the Saiyyads was 150,000 slaves, therefore the total number of captives comes to 750,000.[18]

What can be said? The great tragedy is that they all died in vain. There is no room for the story of the victims in the modern study of slavery.

SLAVERY TODAY

The practice of Islamic slavery is alive and well today. In 1983 the Sudan became an Islamic state with Sharia law. The Muslims have brutalized the Christians and other religious followers. Even the UN has documented the slavery in the Sudan. Islam in the Sudan has shown a creative approach to genocide. The government is slowly starving the population. The army attacks villages, kill the old and young, then captures the healthy Kafirs for slaves:

> Thousands of men, women and children are captured when their villages are surrounded, or are snatched while tending their crops, herding their animals, or collecting water. Many people run to hide in caves to escape government attacks, but they are driven even from these refuges by hunger and thirst, or by attacks using tear gas. Captives are taken to garrisons, forced to carry their own looted possessions, or drive their own stolen animals in front of them. These captives—or 'returnees', as the government calls them—usually never see their families or villages again. Many are tortured. Women are raped and forced to work, often in special labour camps. All but the youngest children are separated for 'schooling'—i.e. conversion to Islam [Facing Genocide: The Nuba of Sudan, published by African Rights on 21 July 1995].

The government uses food as a means for luring Sudanese Christians into its "peace camps" located in the desert. Food distribution is carried out by Islamic organizations. They use the promise of food as a means of converting Christians and animists to Islam. The technique is very simple: if one does not bear an Islamic name, one is denied food. Without any means of alternative support the choice is Islam or death (Sabit A. Alley's paper delivered at the 19th Annual Holocaust and Genocide Program, Institute for Holocaust and Genocide Studies, March 17, 2001).

In Mauritania, slavery is openly practiced. Arab-Mauritanians hold an estimated half million slaves. Female slaves have their clitorises removed. No child can be in school without a Muslim name.

---

18. K.S. Lal, *Muslim Slave System in Medieval India*, Voice of Dharma, 1994.

THE DHIMMITUDE OF THE KAFIR

Historically, Muslims are dominant to every other demographic group. No one is lower than a slave. No one is higher than the slave's master. For 1400 years Islam has enslaved African, Asians, Christians, Hindus, Buddhists, Europeans and even Americans. On the other hand, no one enslaves Muslims, unless the African slaver runs out of Kafirs. But even then, it is a Muslim who enslaves the Muslim.

The absolute dominance of Muslims is shown by the fact that no one blames them or holds them responsible for slavery. Islam not only enslaves the bodies of the Kafirs, but enslaves the minds of the Kafir intellectuals. One of the most forbidden topics to be discussed is the role of Islam in slavery, both today and throughout the last 1400 years.

As a cruel example of how the Kafir mind submits to Islam regarding slavery, go to an event where freed slaves from Africa or the "Lost Boys" of the Sudan are featured. Money is raised, sympathy is given and not one word about Islam is ever mentioned. Slavery just happens. We get to see an effect without a cause, an impossibility, but a pseudo-reality, nevertheless.

This mental submission of the Kafir to Islam is called dhimmitude. There are three ways to submit to the duality of Islam. The first is to be a Muslim. The second is to be a slave. But Mohammed invented a third way of submission—the dhimmi. The dhimmi was invented when Mohammed conquered the Jews of Khaybar. They could still be Jews in the privacy of their homes, but all public space became Islamic. The government, taxes, and laws were Islamic.

When the Kafir lets Islam have its way in public affairs, the Kafir becomes a dhimmi. When Kafirs teach about slavery and don't teach about Islam and slavery, the Kafir is a dhimmi. When the university curriculum about "gender studies" does not include the servitude of the Islamic woman, the mind set of the curriculum is dhimmitude. When the rabbi or the minister says that they worship the same god as the Muslim, but have never read the Trilogy, the rabbi and the ministers are dhimmis. When the media reports or talks about Islam and has no knowledge about the doctrine or history of political Islam, they are dhimmis.

THE SIRA

CHAPTER 6

*8:13 This [Allah cast terror into the Kafir's heart] was because
they opposed Allah and His messenger. Ones who oppose
Allah and His messenger will be severely punished by Allah.*

The Sira is Mohammed's life as recorded by Ibn Ishaq. It is the defini-
tive biography. It is primarily about jihad. Over 75% of the text is about a
political struggle, raids, battles and theft. It is jihad that produces slavery.

The Sira gives a context to Islam. Without the Sira and the Hadith,
there is no Islam. Without the story of Mohammed, the Koran is incom-
prehensible and meaningless.

Mohammed went from being a preacher to a politician and warrior. As
a preacher he garnered only 150 followers in 13 years. Then he changed
Islam's strategy into a political form. After 10 years of jihad—holy war—
Mohammed became the first ruler of all of Arabia and he did not have a
single opponent left alive in Arabia. He was completely and totally politically triumphant.

Part of that rise to power was fueled by the money of the slave trade.
This version of the Sira condenses Mohammed's career and shows how
slaves played a part in it.

If the paragraph is about slaves there is this symbol in the margin.   §

CHILDHOOD

Mohammed's father was called Abdullah, meaning slave of Allah. Allah
was a high god of the many gods worshiped in the town of Mecca. His
father died while his mother was pregnant. When he was five years old,
his mother died and his grandfather took over his upbringing. Then Mohammed was orphaned for the third time when his grandfather died and
his raising was assumed by his uncle, Abu Talib. All were of the Quraysh
tribe. These brief facts are the history known about his early childhood.

I115[1] When Mohammed was eight years old, his grandfather died. He
was then taken in by Abu Talib, his uncle. His uncle took him on a trading trip to Syria, which was a very different place from Mecca. Syria was
a sophisticated Christian country very much a part of the cosmopolitan

---

1.   The number is a reference to Ishaq's , the Sira.

culture of the Mediterranean. It was Syrian Christians who gave the Arabs their alphabet. When Mohammed was a child, there had never been a book written in Arabic. Only poems and business correspondence were written in Arabic.

MARRIAGE

1120 When Mohammed was grown, he was hired by the wealthy widow, Khadija, a distant cousin, to act as her agent in trading with Syria. Mohammed had a reputation of good character and good business sense. Trading between Mecca and Syria was risky business because it took skill to manage a caravan and to make the best deal in Syria.

§ 1120 On one trip Mohammed took one of Khadija's slaves along. When they returned, the slave related a story that a Christian had said Mohammed was destined to be a man of power. On the same trip Mohammed managed to double Khadija's investment. She proposed marriage to him. They married and had six children, two sons who died in childhood, and four daughters who lived to adulthood.

1150 Mohammed would take month-long retreats to be alone and practice the Quraysh religion. After the retreat he would go and circumambulate (circle and pray) the Kabah.

1152 At the age of forty Mohammed began to have visions and hear voices. His visions were first shown to him as bright as daybreak during his sleep in the month of Ramadan. Mohammed said that the angel, Gabriel, came to him with a brocade with writing on it and commanded him to read.

THE FIRST CONVERT

1156 Mohammed's wife was the first convert. From the beginning, she had encouraged and believed him. She knew that he was of good character and did not think him to be deceived or crazy.

Soon he stopped hearing voices or seeing visions, became depressed and felt abandoned. Then his visions started again.

EARLY ISLAM

The idea of having an Arabian prophet was new. The sources of the native religions were unknown, but the new religion of Islam had a self-declared prophet. The Jews had prophets, and now the Arabs had their own prophet in Mohammed. The religion was called Islam, meaning submission. Those who joined Islam were called Muslims, meaning those who submitted.

I161 A new element was added to the religion. Any person who rejected the revelations of Mohammed would be eternally punished. Only Islam was acceptable.

I178 Fortunately for Mohammed, the Arabs of Medina were attracted to Islam's message. Since half of their town consisted of Jews, the Arabs of Medina were used to the concept of only one god.

PUBLIC PREACHING

At first Mohammed only told close friends and relatives about his message. Then he began to preach more publicly. The Koran condemns those who argue with Mohammed, since to argue against Islam is to be an enemy of Allah. The Koran gives an exact accounting of the arguments of the opponents of Mohammed.

The Meccans reasoned that if the all-knowing god of the universe was the author of the Koran, then why did he not deliver the entire Koran at once, instead of delivering it a piece at a time.

I183 Mohammed continued to preach the glory of Allah and condemn the Quraysh religion. He told them their way of life was wrong and their ancestors would burn in Hell. He cursed their gods, disparaged their religion and divided the community, setting one tribesman against another. The Quraysh felt that this was unbearable. Tolerance had always been their way. There were many clans, many gods, many religions. Another religion was fine, why did Mohammed demean the other religions?

I206 Some of the first Muslims were slaves and the Meccans prosecuted §
them when they could. Abu Bakr was a wealthy man and bought and freed six Muslim slaves to stop their persecution.

I260 There was one Christian in Mecca in whom Mohammed took an §
interest. He was a Christian slave who ran a booth in the market. Mohammed would go and speak with him at length. This led to the Quraysh claiming that what Mohammed said in the Koran, came from the Christian slave.

THE NIGHT JOURNEY

I264 One night as he lay sleeping, Mohammed said that the angel nudged him with his foot. Mohammed awoke. They went out the door and found a white animal, half mule and half donkey. Its feet had wings and could move to the horizon at one step. Gabriel put Mohammed on the white animal and off they went to Jerusalem to the site of the Temple.

I264 There at the temple were Jesus, Abraham, Moses, and other prophets. Mohammed led them in prayer. Gabriel brought Mohammed two bowls. One was filled with wine and the other was filled with milk. Mohammed took the one with milk and drank it. That was the right choice.

1265 Aisha, Mohammed's favorite wife, used to say that Mohammed never left the bed that night, however, his spirit soared. When Mohammed went out into Mecca to tell the story of his Night Journey, the owner of the home that Mohammed in which Mohammed had slept in sent her black, female slave to follow Mohammed and see how the Meccans reacted to his story.

1272 Mohammed continued to preach Islam and condemn the old Arabic religions. There were those of the Quraysh who defended their culture and religion and argued with him. Mohammed called them mockers and cursed one of them, "Oh Allah, blind him and kill his son."MOHAMMED'S PROTECTOR AND WIFE BOTH DIE

1278 Mohammed's protector was his uncle, Abu Talib. When Abu Talib fell ill, some of the leaders of the Quraysh came to his bedside. They said to him, " Please work out a compromise between Mohammed and us."

1278 So Abu Talib called Mohammed to his side. "Nephew, these men have come so that you can give them something and they can give you something." Mohammed said, "If they will give me one word, they can rule the Persians and the Arabs. And they must accept Allah as their Lord and renounce their gods."

1278 Mohammed turned his attention to his dying uncle. He asked him to become a Muslim and then Mohammed could intercede for him on judgment day. His uncle died as a Kafir.

MARRIAGE

M113[2] About three months after the death of Khadija Mohammed married Sauda, a widow and a Muslim.

M113 Abu Bakr had a daughter, Aisha, who was six years old. Soon after marrying Sauda, Mohammed was betrothed to Aisha, who was to become his favorite wife. The consummation of the marriage would not take place until she turned nine.

1279 With Abu Talib's death, Mohammed needed political allies. Mohammed went to the city of Taif, about fifty miles away, with one servant. In Taif he met with three brothers who were politically powerful. Mohammed called them to Islam and asked them to help him in his struggles with those who would defend their native religions.

His trip was a failure and he returned to Mecca.

---

2   The M refers to the page of Sir William Muir's

THE BEGINNING OF POWER AND JIHAD IN MEDINA

Medina was about a ten-day journey from Mecca, but since ancient times the Medinans had come to Mecca for the fairs. Medina was half Jewish and half Arabian, and there was an ongoing tension between the two. The Jews worked as farmers and craftsmen and were literate. They were the wealthy class, but their power was slowly waning. In times past the Arabs had raided and stolen from the Jews who retaliated by saying that one day a prophet would come and lead them to victory over the Arabs. In spite of the tensions, the Arab tribe of Khazraj were allied with them.

I304 Back in Medina the Muslims now practiced their new religion openly. But most of the Arabs still practiced their ancient tribal religions. The Muslims would desecrate the old shrines and ritual objects. They would even break into houses and steal ritual objects and throw them into the latrines. On one occasion they killed a dog and tied the dog's body to a ritual object and thew it into the latrine.

IMMIGRATION

I314 The Muslim Medinans had pledged to support Mohammed in war and to help the Muslims from Mecca. The Muslims in Mecca left and went to Medina. The Muslims from both Mecca and Medina were about to be tested.

Mohammed was one of the last to leave Mecca for Medina. In Medina Mohammed built the first mosque. There were now two types of Muslims in Medina. The native Medinan Muslims were called the Helpers, and the new arrivals were called the Immigrants.

THE COVENANT

Mohammed drew up a political charter that included the basis of war. The Jews were included in the charter as allies of the Muslims. Mohammed was to be the arbitrator in disputes.

MARRIAGE

M177 About seven months after arriving in Medina, Mohammed, aged fifty-three, consummated his marriage with Aisha, now age nine. She moved out of her father's house into what was to become a compound of apartments adjoining the mosque. She was allowed to bring her dolls into the harem due to her age.

THE JEWS

In Mecca, Mohammed had divided the community into Muslims and those practicing the native Arabic religions. In Mecca he adopted all the classical Jewish stories to prove his prophecies and spoke well of the Jews. However, there were almost no Jews living in Mecca, and therefore, no one to differ with him.

In Medina, half of the population were Jews who let Mohammed know they disagreed with him. So in Medina, Mohammed argued with Jews as well as the Kafir Arabs. Even though there were very few in the town who were Christian, Mohammed argued against them as well. All Kafirs were verbally attacked in Medina.

1415 Thirteen years after he started preaching and one year after going to Medina, Mohammed began to prepare for war as commanded by Allah. He would fight his enemies: the Kafirs.

THE FIRST RAIDS

1416-423 Mohammed sent his fighters out on seven armed raids to find a trade caravan headed to Mecca.

On the eighth try the jihadists found the caravan. They killed one man and captured the rest. The booty and captives were taken back to Medina. There was a small problem. They had raided and killed someone in a sacred month of peace. This violated Arabic tribal custom.

But the Koran said that killing the Kafirs in the sacred months was a moral act. For the Meccans to resist Islam was an offence against Allah, so the killing was justified.

FIGHTING IN ALLAH'S CAUSE—BADR

The next Meccan caravan was large. When the Meccans got wind that the Muslims were going to attack, they sent out a small army to protect it. Mohammed sent out his men to either attack the caravan or do battle with the protecting army.

1433 Mohammed and his men headed out of Medina for what would prove to be one of the most important battles in all of history, a battle that would change the world forever.

1435 Mohammed was cheered. He said, "I see the enemy dead on the ground." They headed towards Badr and camped near there for the night. He sent several scouts to the well at Badr and the scouts found two slaves with water camels. They felt sure they were from the caravan and brought back them back to Mohammed. Two of Mohammed's men questioned them as Mohammed was nearby praying. Mohammed wanted to know which group they were facing—the Quraysh caravan or the army under Abu Sufyan. The men replied that they were from the Quraysh. While Mohammed prayed, his men began to beat them and torture the captured slaves.

1436 Mohammed told his men that the slaves told them the truth until 8 they started to beat and torture them. Then the slaves had lied but it had been the lie that the Muslims wanted to hear. Mohammed asked the slaves how many of the Meccan army there were and who were the leaders? When they told him, he was delighted and told his warriors that Mecca had sent their best men to be slaughtered.

1440-444 The Meccans marched forth at daybreak. The battle began. Before Islam the killing of kin and tribal brothers had been forbidden since the dawn of time. After Islam, brother would kill brother and sons would kill their fathers, fighting in Allah's cause—jihad.

Victory was complete. Although the Muslims were outnumbered two to one, they were victorious.

1459 They set off for Medina with the spoils of war and the prisoners to be ransomed, except for one who had spoken against Mohammed. He was brought in front of the Prophet to be killed, but before the sword struck, he asked, "Who will care for my family?"

M230 The Prophet replied, "Hell!" After he fell dead, Mohammed said, "Unbeliever in Allah and his Prophet and his Book! I give thanks to Allah Who has killed you and made my eyes satisfied."

1481 After war and victory there were the spoils of war to divide. One fifth went to the Apostle, Allah's prophet.

Mohammed left Mecca as a preacher and prophet. He entered Medina with about 150 Muslim converts. After a year in Medina there were about 250-300 Muslims and most of them were very poor. After the battle of Badr, a new Islam emerged. Mohammed rode out of Medina as a politician and general. Islam became an armed political force with a religious motivation, jihad.

THE JEWS

When Mohammed arrived in Medina about half the town were Jews. There were three tribes of Jews and two tribes of Arabs. Almost none of the Jews had Hebrew names. They were Arabs to some degree. At the same time many of the Arabs' religious practices contained elements of Judaism. The Jews were farmers and tradesmen and lived in their own fortified quarters. In general, they were better educated and more prosperous than the Arabs.

Before Mohammed arrived, there had been bad blood and killing among the tribes. The last battle had been fought between the two Arab tribes, but each of the Jewish tribes had joined the battle with their particular Arab allies. In addition to that tension between the two Arab tribes, there was a tension between the Jews and the Arabs. The division of the Jews and fighting on different sides was condemned by Mohammed. The Torah preached that the Jews should be unified, and they failed in this.

All of these quarrelsome tribal relationships were one reason that Mohammed was invited to Medina, but the result was further polarization, not unity. The new split was between Islam and those Arabs and their Jewish partners who resisted Islam.

I351 About this time, the leaders of the Jews spoke out against Mohammed. The rabbis began to ask him difficult questions. Doubts and questions arose about his doctrine. But for Mohammed, doubts about Allah were evil. However, two of the Jewish Arabs joined with Mohammed as Muslims. They believed him when he said that he was the Jewish prophet that came to fulfill the Torah.

THE REAL TORAH IS IN THE KORAN

Mohammed said repeatedly that the Jews and Christians corrupted their sacred texts in order to conceal the fact that he was prophesied in their scriptures. The stories in the Koran are similar to those of the Jew's scriptures, but they make different points. In the Koran, all of the stories found in Jewish scripture indicated that Allah destroyed those cultures that did not listen to their messengers. According to Mohammed, the scriptures of the Jews had been changed to hide the fact that Islam is the true religion and that he was the last prophet of the Jews.

AN OMINOUS CHANGE

I381 In Mecca, Mohammed spoke well of the Jews, who were very few. In Medina there were many Jews and his relations with them were tense. Up to now Mohammed had led prayer facing in the direction of Jerusalem. Now the *kiblah*, direction of prayer, was changed to the Kabah in Mecca. Some of the Jews came to him and asked why he had changed the direction of prayer. After all, he said that he followed the religion of Abraham.

THE AFFAIR OF THE JEWS OF QAYNUQA

I545 There were three tribes of Jews in Medina. The Beni Qaynuqa were goldsmiths and lived in a stronghold in their quarters. It is said by

Mohammed that they broke the treaty that had been signed when Mohammed came to Medina. How they did this is unclear.

1546 Some time later Mohammed besieged the Beni Qaynuqa Jews in their quarters. Neither of the other two Jewish tribes came to their support. Finally the Jews surrendered, expecting to be slaughtered after their capture.

But one of the Jews' old allies persuaded Mohammed not to kill them. Mohammed exiled the Jews and took all of their wealth and goods.

JIHAD, A SETBACK

The Meccans had lost at the battle of Badr, but they raised an army and returned to fight the Muslims at Uhud, near Medina.

1560 When they saw the Meccans, Mohammed said, "Let there be no fighting until I give the word." Mohammed placed 50 archers to protect his rear and flank. They must not move but hold that ground.

1562 The morrow came and the battle was to begin.

1557 Hind, a Meccan woman, had a black slave called Washi, who was an expert with the javelin. She told Washi that if he could kill Hamza ɡ [Hamza had killed Hind's uncle at Badr] he would give him his freedom. On the way to the battle, whenever Hind saw Washi, she would say, "Come on, you father of blackness, satisfy your vengeance and ours."

1557 During the battle Washi hung near the edge of the fighting and looked for Hamza. Hamza fought like a lion as Washi watched. As Hamza fought one of the Meccans, he said, "Come here, you son of a clitoris cutter. " Hamza then killed the man whose mother performed the female circumcision [removed the girl's clitoris, common surgery in Arabia.] Then Washi threw his javelin and killed Hamza. Washi was now free and left the field.

The Muslims lost because the archers did not hold their position, and instead they ran to the Meccan camp to steal their goods.

The Meccans won, but they did not press their advantage and let Mohammed escape.

1606 The Koran said that the success that the Kafirs experienced was temporary. They would grow in their evil and be punished. Allah would not leave the believers in this state. But this trial would separate the weak from the strong. Those who have wealth should spend it on jihad.

THE RAID ON THE MUSTALIQ TRIBE

1725 When Mohammed heard that the Arab tribe, the Mustaliq, were opposed to him and were gathering against him, he set out with his army to attack. He found them at a watering hole and combat started. Islam was victorious and the Mustaliq and their women, children, and goods were taken as spoils of war and distributed to the fighters.

1729 The captives of the tribe of Mustaliq were parceled out as spoils. There was a ransom price set upon their heads. If the ransom were not ǧ paid then the people were treated as spoils and slaves.

1729 This marriage had a side effect. The captives were now related to Mohammed's wife. They were all released without ransom.

CLEANSING

Mohammed attacked the second of the two Jewish tribes in Medina. The Jews would not admit that he was a real prophet and for this they would pay. Mohammed put the Jews under siege and burned their date palm plantations. The other Jews would not help them. They cut a deal and got to leave alive with all they could carry.

Since there was no actual fighting and the jihadists did no work, Mohammed got all of the booty.

The burning of the date palms violated Arabic tribal customs. But the Koran said that it was a moral act against the Kafir Jews.

THE BATTLE OF THE TRENCH

The Meccans came back to Medina to fight against Islam. But Mohammed had spies in Mecca, so he knew they were coming. At the suggestion of a Muslim who had been to Persia, the Muslims built a defensive trench.

1677-683 Mohammed was able to use his agents to sow discord among those allied against him. The trench defense frustrated the Meccans. The weather was bad, and the allies were distrustful of each other. In terms of actual combat only a handful of men were killed over the twenty-day siege. The Meccans broke camp and went back home. It was a victory for Mohammed.

THE SOLUTION FOR THE JEWS

Mohammed put the Jews under siege. They surrendered and submitted to the judgment of Saed, an old ally.

1688 The Jews decided to let a Muslim they thought was their friend, Saed, deliver judgment if they surrendered to Mohammed. Saed's judgment was simple. Kill all the men. Take their property and take the women ǧ and children as slaves. Mohammed said, "You have given the judgment of Allah."

1690 The captives were taken into Medina. They dug trenches in the market place of Medina. It was a long day, but 800 Jews were beheaded that day. Mohammed and his twelve-year-old wife, Aisha, sat and watched the slaughter the entire day and into the night. The Apostle of Allah had every male Jew killed.

1693 Mohammed took the property, wives and children of the Jews, and divided it up amongst the Muslims. Mohammed took his one-fifth of the slaves and sent a Muslim with the female Jewish slaves to a nearby city g where the women were sold for pleasure. Mohammed invested the money from the sale of the female slaves for horses and weapons.

TREATY OF AL HUDAYBIYA

Mohammed decided it was time for the Muslims to make a pilgrimage to Mecca and the Kabah. But the Meccans would not let the Muslims enter, even though they were unarmed and in pilgrimage clothing. So Mohammed parlayed with the Meccans.

1747 They drew up a treaty to the effect that there would be no war for ten years, there would be no hostilities, and no one could convert to Islam without their guardians' permission. In turn the Muslims could come next year and stay for three days in Mecca, but they could not enter this year.

1748 Many of the Muslims were depressed. Mohammed had promised that they could enter Mecca. Now they could not. Before they left they sacrificed the camels and shaved their heads, doing as many of the rituals as they could without getting into Mecca.

KHAYBAR

1756 After the treaty of Al Hudaybiya, Mohammed stayed in Medina for about two months before he collected his army and marched to the forts of Khaybar, a community of wealthy Jewish farmers who lived in a village of separate forts about 100 miles from Medina.

1758 Mohammed seized the forts one at a time. Among the captives was a beautiful Jewess named Safiya. Mohammed took her for his sexual pleasure. One of his men had first chosen her for his own slave of pleasure, but Mohammed traded him two of her cousins for Safiya. Mohammed always got first choice of the spoils of war and the women.

1759 On the occasion of Khaybar, Mohammed put forth new orders g about sex with captive women. If the woman was pregnant, she was not to be used for sex until after the birth of the child. Nor were any women to be used for sex who were unclean with regards to the Muslim laws about menstruation.

1764 Mohammed knew that there was a large treasure hidden somewhere in Khaybar, so he brought forth the Jew who he thought knew the most about it and questioned him. The Jew denied any knowledge. Mohammed told one of his men, "Torture the Jew until you extract what he has." So the Jew was staked on the ground, and a small fire built on his chest to get him to talk. When the man was nearly dead and still would not talk, Mohammed had him released and taken to one of his men whose brother had been killed in the fight. This Muslim got the pleasure of cutting off the tortured Jew's head.

1763 Mohammed had his freed slave, Bilal, to go and get the two best looking women and bring them to him. Bilal brought the women past the dead Jews. One of them began to shriek and pour dust on her head. Mohammed said, "Take this she-devil away from me." Then he threw his mantle over Safiya so that the men would know that she was his. Mohammed then told Bilal, "Do you not have any compassion, bringing these two women past their dead husbands?"

1764 At Khaybar Mohammed instituted the first dhimmis. After the best of the goods were taken from the Jews, Mohammed left them to work the land. Since his men knew nothing about farming, and the Jews were skilled at it, they worked the land and gave Mohammed half of their profits.

MECCA CONQUERED

The treaty of Hudaybiya was broken by a fight between allies of Mohammed and allies of Mecca. Mohammed took advantage of this and attacked Mecca.

1811 As a result of the fighting between a tribe allied with the Meccans and a tribe allied with Mohammed, he marched on Mecca with 10,000 men to punish them.

The Meccans decided to yield without a fight. The Meccan leader submitted to Islam. The leader went ahead and announced to the citizens that Mohammed's army was coming. They were not to resist but to go into their houses, his house or the Kabah and that they would be safe.

1819 Mohammed had told his commanders only to kill those who resisted. Otherwise they were to bother no one except for those who had spoken against Mohammed. The list of those to be killed:

- One of Mohammed's secretaries, who had said that when he was recording Mohammed's Koranic revelations sometimes Mohammed let the secretary insert better speech. This caused him to lose faith and he became an apostate (left Islam).

- Two singing girls who had sung satires against Mohammed.
- A Muslim tax collector who had become an apostate.
- A man who had insulted Mohammed.

1821 Mohammed went to the Kabah, prayed and then destroyed all of the religious art in Mecca.

BATTLE OF TAIF

1872 Mohammed attacked al Taif, a walled town. The Muslims pitched their tents near the walls and settled down for a siege. Mohammed had brought two wives and put them into two tents. The battle did not go well and the town was successful in resisting jihad. Mohammed had the fighters destroy all of their vineyards.

1873 One of the Muslim women asked Mohammed if she could have the jewelry of two of the richest women in Taif. Mohammed said she could but he doubted that they were going to succeed. Shortly after that he called off the attack. On the way back, one of the Muslims said that he did not mind losing the battle, but he did regret not getting a woman from Taif for a slave. The people of Taif were noted for their intelligence and he wanted to breed the slave to have smart children from her. $

THE HAWAZIN

1877 The Hawazin had been beaten by the Muslims. As Mohammed came back from Taif, he stopped to deal with them. They had submitted to Islam and wanted relief from their loss. Their leaders pointed out to Mohammed that some of his prisoners were members of his foster family. Mohammed gave the leaders a choice. They could have their cattle and goods back or their wives and sons back. They choose their families.

1878 Mohammed gave three of his companions a slave girl for each to use for sex. Uthman took his sex slave and gave her to his son. $

THE RAID ON TABUK

1894 Mohammed decided to raid the Byzantines. Normally he never let his men actually know where he was headed. He would announce a destination, but after they were on the way, he would announce the actual target. This raid was far away and the weather was very hot, so greater preparations had to be made. The men began to prepare, but with no enthusiasm because of the heat. It was time for the harvest to begin, and they remembered the last combat with the Byzantines where they lost badly.

THE FAREWELL PILGRIMAGE

1968 Ten years after entering Medina, Mohammed made what was to be his last pilgrimage to Mecca. There he made his farewell address:

1969 The men have rights over their wives and the wives have rights over the men. The wives must never commit adultery nor act in a sexual manner towards others. If they do, put them in separate rooms and beat them lightly. If they refrain from these things, they have the right to food and clothing. Lay injunctions on women lightly for they are prisoners of the men and have no control over their persons.

§   M473 Feed and clothe your slaves well.

THE FINAL STATE OF CHRISTIANS AND JEWS

M453 When Mohammed first started preaching in Mecca, his religion was Arabian. Then Allah became identified with Jehovah and Jewish elements were introduced. When Mohammed moved to Medina, he argued with the Jews when they denied his status as a prophet in the Judaic line. He then annihilated the Jews.

M453 In his last statement, Jews and Christians became perpetual second class political citizens, dhimmis. Only those Christians and Jews who submit to Islam are protected. The real Christians are those who deny the Trinity and accept Mohammed as the final prophet. The real Jews are those who accept Mohammed as the final prophet of their god, Jehovah. Both Christians and Jews must accept that the Koran is the true Scripture and that the Old Testament and New Testament are corrupt and in error. All other Jews and Christians are false and Kafirs.

> Koran 9:29 *Make war on those who have received the Scriptures [Jews and Christians] but do not believe in Allah or in the Last Day. They do not forbid what Allah and His Messenger have forbidden. The Christians and Jews do not follow the religion of truth until they submit and pay the poll tax [jizya], and they are humiliated.*

The Christians have hidden their prophesies that Mohammed would come to fulfill the work of Christ. To believe in the divinity of Christ is to refuse to submit to Islam. Like the Jews, only those Christians who submit to Islam, honor Mohammed as their last prophet, become dhimmis and are ruled by the Sharia (Islamic law) are actual Christians. Islam defines all religions. All religions must submit to Islam.

SUMMARY OF MOHAMMED'S ARMED EVENTS

I973 In a nine year period Mohammed personally took part in twenty-seven raids. There were thirty-eight other battles and expeditions. This is a total of sixty-five armed events, not including assassinations and executions, for an average of one armed event every six weeks.

MOHAMMED'S DEATH

I1006 Mohammed grew ill, weakened and was in a great deal of pain. Later he died with his head in Aisha's lap. His final words were the perfect summation of Islam, political action based upon religion.

> B4,52,288 *Mohammed said, "There should be no other religions besides Islam in Arabia" and that money should continue to be paid to influence the foreign, Kafir ambassadors.*

T1831 Mohammed was buried beneath his bed. The bed was removed and a grave was dug where it had stood.

This is the Sunna of Mohammed

COMMENTS

CHAPTER 7

SUBMISSION

The Islamic slave doctrine is based upon submission. Submission is always about the master/slave relationship. Allah is the master of the Muslim slaves. The Muslim is the master of the dhimmi slaves. The Muslim male is the master of the Muslim female. And the Muslim is the slave master of all slaves, in particular, the African slaves today. In submission, there is always a master and a slave.

It is obvious to the casual observer that slavery rests upon ethical duality and submission. The object of slavery must be less than human, a Kafir.

Mohammed used slavery because it worked and it was as Arabic as sand. Mohammed's life was infused with slavery. His pulpit was build by a slave, a slave gave him a son, a slave cooked his food, cut his hair, and made his clothes. The money from slavery gave Mohammed more material for war, so he could get more slaves. Slaves were the lifeblood of Islam. And Mohammed, the white man, owned both male and female black slaves.

Mohammed's attitude was pure dualism. He preached freeing slaves after they converted to Islam, while he killed others to make more slaves. He preached being good to slaves while he organized rapes of the new slaves. Mohammed never expressed the slightest doubt about the ethics of enslavement of others.

MOLESTATION OF THE MIND

The Kafirs accept violence and threats from Islam without protest. This acceptance of violence is the sign of a profoundly molested psyche. The Kafirs are like the battered wife and molested child of Islam.

Violent molestation can cause denial.

Islam's explosive jihad and the application of Sharia destroyed half of Christianity, Hinduism, and Buddhism. Now let's look at what manifests after violent molestation. The *YWCA Rape Crisis Counselor Training Manual* shows the following reactions are common among victims of rape and child molestation:

Disbelief: the victim has an incredibly hard time believing that the attacks took place.

The media reports very little of the jihad around the world and never connects the dots between the violent events.

Fear: fear is the tool that the abuser uses to control the victim.

Islam has used fear against the Kafirs since its beginning. The first person Mohammed had assassinated was a poetess who mocked him. Any public critic of Islam lives in fear. The Kafir society will not protect their critic out of dhimmitude.

Guilt: the victim finds a way to blame himself/herself.

It is our fault. We have not treated Islam in the right way.

Branded: the victim does not want others to find out about the crime.

We do not teach the history of Islamic slavery and the deaths of 120 million Africans or a million Europeans taken as slaves by Islam. We do not teach the history of the jihad against Hindus, Christians, or Buddhists.

Lack of control: during the attack the victim was helpless. This helplessness extends to dealing with the problem.

Where is the person who is optimistic about what can be done to deal with political Islam?

Powerlessness: things will not get better.

Pessimism about dealing with Islam is the prevailing attitude.

The Abuser

The traits and characteristics of the abuser are well documented.

Denial: the abuser denies that the abuse ever took place.

Muslims do not acknowledge any of the crimes committed in the name of Islam. Islam denies its history in slavery.

Inadequacy: Abusers are arrogant and overly self-confident.

Islam is never wrong. Muslims are the best of people according to the Koran.

Domination

The word islam means "submit." The abuser expects submission on the part of the victim, the Kafir.

Inability to understand or recognize the problem: the abuser is the last person to admit he has a problem.

Islam has never accepted any responsibility for its 1400 year history of slavery.

Manipulation: the abuser wants to make the victim feel guilty.

Islam is presented as the victim. After every jihad-terror attack, the cry goes out: "Oh, the poor Muslims will be hated and reviled."

Obsessed with weapons

Have you ever noticed all the swords on Islamic flags and seals? The AK-47 rifle thrust in the air is a symbol of Islam.

The Kafir world, in particular its intellectuals, are classic manifestations of the abused wife and the abused child. The dhimmi is a broken person and doesn't even know it. Can we say that we fit the abused child profile?

INTELLECTUALS AS ISLAM'S MOLESTED CHILDREN

The Western intellectual has always been ineffectual in resisting Islam. The roots of Western thought about Islam are found in the rapid conquest of half of Western culture 1,400 areas ago. Jihad exploded when the Roman/Byzantine empire was in decay. The West, weak and enfeebled, reeled from overwhelming shock when its culture was destroyed, creating a foundation of fear and denial. This fear manifested in the failure of the Western intellectual to even name the enemy. When you read early Western accounts of that time, you never read of Islam or jihad. All references are to Arabs, Turks, and Moors. There was never a real understanding of political Islam's foundations.

Ignorance

In the late 18th century, scholars studied a weakened Islam that was exotic and romantic. Modern historians shows no horror at Islam's bloodshed, rape, enslavement, and destruction of cultures. History almost seems written with the assistance of opiates; all the victims' suffering is vague. The intellectuals are disconnected and in total denial. The Western attitude towards Islam results from an intellectual molestation.

In *Foreign Affairs* and other intellectual journals, the analysis of Islamic politics is devoid of any reference to the foundational documents of Islam, the history of jihad, and Islamic foreign policy. All the analysis is purely Western in nature and completely disregards the core values of Islamic politics. The only intellectual criticism is self-criticism, never criticism of political Islam.

Imbalance

Why have intellectuals sliced-and-diced the Bible and Christ but uttered nary a critical word about the Koran and Mohammed? Where is the technical and systemic analysis of the Koran as though it is just another historical document? Find one critical paper of thought about Islam at

Harvard. Why are all university opinions of Islam written or vetted by Muslim scholars?

Fear

Every single artist and intellectual who opposed Mohammed was killed or fled Arabia. Intellectuals in both Europe and America have been threatened and murdered. Theo van Gogh, Pim Fortuyn, Salman Rushdie, the Danish cartoonists who lampooned Mohammed and Ayaan Hirsi Ali are forgotten victims.

How refreshing it would be if even one college professor or media writer ever hinted that this type of action was wrong. How remarkable it would be if media criticized the Islamic threats and murder of intellectuals. The Mohammed cartoon riots showed how afraid intellectuals are of Islam. They are willing to do anything to appease the abuser. If Islam objects to political cartoons, then the media will find some imagined high moral ground in submitting to Islam's demands to end freedom of the press.

The Kafir intellectuals are the molested children of Islam who deny the history of Islam and are ignorant of the doctrine of political Islam.

BLACKS AS ISLAM'S MOLESTED CHILDREN

The accepted history of race in the U.S. is that white men captured Africans, brought them to the U.S. and sold them as slaves. When the white slavers showed up on the west coast of Africa, they didn't capture Africans. They looked them over in the pens, gave the African slave traders their money, took their bills of sale, and loaded their purchases into boats.

The African slave traders were Muslims. Their ancestors had been plying the trade of war, capture, enslavement, and sale for a thousand years. Mohammed was a slave trader. Long after the white slave traders quit, the Muslims continued their African slave trade. It still exists today.

Blacks define themselves on the basis of slavery. They will not go beyond the white, Christian version of slavery. There is only one theory of history—the West African Limited Edition version of history. There is no admission of the broad scope of slave history. Hindu slavery? It never happened. White and European slavery? It never happened. Slavery on the East coast of Africa? It never happened. A massive slave trade through the Sahara into North Africa? It never happened. Black, eunuch slaves at the Medina mosque? It never happened.

What about modern Africa? How can black leaders not see how Islam carries out its sacred violence? Why aren't the black columnists, writers, professors, or ministers speaking out? They are in total denial. They are the molested children of Islam.

There is a small modern story that illustrates the black, molested mind. A black man was born and given the name of his father, who was named after a white slavery abolitionist, Cassius Clay. After Cassius Clay became the world's heavy-weight boxing champion, he became a Muslim. He then took the name, Mohammed Ali. He dropped the name of a white abolitionist to take the name of two Arab slave traders, Mohammed and Ali. Only a molested mind would be so proud of so great an error.

Blacks are dhimmis and serve Islam by being quiet. There is a deep fear of Islam that makes them overlook and placate Islam. Arabs are the master of blacks.

One thing whites and blacks have in common is that their ancestors were enslaved by Islam, and both are too ignorant to admit it. Molested black and white children of Islam have a secret shame.

FOR MORE INFORMATION

www.politicalislam.com
www.cspii.org
Facebook: @BillWarnerAuthor
Twitter: @politicalislam
YouTube: Political Islam

READING

Slave Soldiers and Islam. Daniel Pipes. Yale University Press.

Muslim Slave System in Medieval India. K. S. Lal. Aditya Prakashan.

Tippu Tip and the East African Slave Trade. Leda Farrant, Hamish Hamilton.

Islam's Black Slaves. Ronald Segal. Farrar, Straus and Giroux.

The African Slave Trade. Basil Davidson. Little, Brown and Company.

Suffering in Africa. James Riley. Clarkson N. Potter.

White Slaves, African Masters. Paul Baepler. University of Chicago Press.

Christian Slaves, Muslim Masters. Robert C. Davis. Pargrave McMillan.

White Gold. Giles Milton. Farrar, Strous and Giroux.

Slaves in Algiers. S. H. Rowson. Copely Publishing Group.

Slavery, Terrorism and Islam. Peter Hammond. Christian Liberty Books.